Crime Pays Off in Reading Delight!

Witness the atrocities of ghoulish multi-murderers whose stories horrified the world.

Learn how some have cheated the gallows—and how courts have condemned and killed the innocent.

Marvel at the machinations of con artists who fleeced their eager victims of millions.

Follow the feats of more-brilliant-than-fiction real-life detectives.

Find out how to protect yourself from mugging, pickpocketing, and burglary.

And enjoy so much more in the grandest tour of the annals of infamy. It's a crime to miss it!

A CATALOGUE OF CRIME

SIGNET and MENTOR Books of Special Interest

- [ ] **COMPUTER CAPERS: Tales of Electronic Thievery, Embezzlement, and Fraud by Thomas Whiteside.** Based on the acclaimed *New Yorker* series, COMPUTER CAPERS chronicles the most spectacular exploits of that new breed, computer criminals—the deviant geniuses who are giving IBM and all the computer experts bad dreams. "A fascinating book . . . a cautionary tale for the age of technology."—*Publishers Weekly* (#ME1753—$2.25)

- [ ] **THE COMPLETE BOOK OF LOCKS, KEYS, BURGLAR AND SMOKE ALARMS, AND OTHER SECURITY DEVICES by Eugene A. Sloane.** Complete with do-it-yourself diagrams and consumer quality and price ratings, this invaluable guide to personal safety tells you everything you need to know to insure that you and your family do not become the helpless victims of today's mounting wave of theft and violence. (#E8713—$2.95)

- [ ] **MONEY MADNESS: The Psychology of Saving, Spending, Loving, and Hating Money by Herb Goldberg, Ph.D., and Robert T. Lewis, Ph.D.** In this fascinating book, two acclaimed psychologists expose all the games that people play by using and abusing money. Learn how money became the most obsessively sought after symbol of success and the ways in which we all seek it, dispose of it, hoard it; and much more. (#E8751—$2.25)*

- [ ] **THE SWISS BANK CONNECTION by Leslie Waller.** This sensational exposé by the bestselling author of THE FAMILY reveals for the first time the full extent of the power of Swiss banks and their connections with the gigantic octopus of organized crime and with the colossal interests of U.S. banks. (#W7375—$1.50)

THE NEW AMERICAN LIBRARY, INC.,
P.O. Box 999, Bergenfield, New Jersey 07621

Please send me the SIGNET and MENTOR BOOKS I have checked above. I am enclosing $_____(please add 50¢ to this order to cover postage and handling). Send check or money order—no cash or C.O.D.'s. Prices and numbers are subject to change without notice.

Name _____

Address _____

City_____ State_____ Zip Code_____

Allow at least 4 weeks for delivery
This offer is subject to withdrawal without notice.

A CATALOGUE OF CRIME

Carl Sifakis

NAL BOOKS ARE ALSO AVAILABLE AT DISCOUNTS IN BULK
QUANTITY FOR INDUSTRIAL OR SALES-PROMOTIONAL USE.
FOR DETAILS, WRITE TO PREMIUM MARKETING DIVISION,
NEW AMERICAN LIBRARY, INC., 1301 AVENUE OF THE
AMERICAS, NEW YORK, NEW YORK 10019.

Copyright © 1979 by Carl Sifakis

All rights reserved

 SIGNET TRADEMARK REG. U.S. PAT. OFF. AND FOREIGN COUNTRIES
REGISTERED TRADEMARK—MARCA REGISTRADA
HECHO EN CHICAGO, U.S.A.

SIGNET, SIGNET CLASSICS, MENTOR, PLUME AND MERIDIAN BOOKS
are published by The New American Library, Inc.,
1301 Avenue of the Americas, New York, New York 10019

First Printing, August, 1979

1 2 3 4 5 6 7 8 9

PRINTED IN THE UNITED STATES OF AMERICA

Contents

I. MASTERS OF THEIR TRADE

Seven Top Public Enemies	2
The All-Time Ten-Most-Wanted List of Murderers, Monsters, and Human Fiends	6
Four Backup Murderers, Monsters, and Human Fiends from the California "Little League"	13
The Three Greatest Swindlers	16
Four Recent "Loner" Assassins and Their Strange "Inferiority"	19
Eight Infamous Lady Killers	20
The Three Most Audacious Crime Plots	26
Hunting for the Forty Notches on Wes Hardin's Gun	28
Five Really Perfect Crimes	32

II. THE MONEY TAKERS

The Money Takers #1	36
The Money Takers #2	36
The Money Takers #3	37
The Money Takers #4	37
The Money Takers #5	38

III. PUNISHMENTS AND EXECUTIONS

Seven First-Night Reviews of the First Electrocution	40
Fourteen Strange Punishments	42
Nine Hanging Dramas	45
Ten Pros and Cons on Capital Punishment	50
Five Mass Murderers and Where They Are Now	51
Six Tombstones That Bespeak Violence	52
Four Thoughts on Hanging	53
Six "Wrong Men"	53

IV. WORDS OF WISDOM

Ten Quotable Quotes	58
Three Famous Denials	59
Fifteen Songs, Odes, Sayings, and Limericks on Crime	59
Eight More Quotable Quotes	61

Twenty-nine Last Words 62

V. INTERESTING METHODS OF SOLVING CRIMES

Six Men Who Had Psychic Experiences and Dreams That Solved Crimes	66
Seven Strange Solutions	72
Five Real-Life Cases for Sherlock Holmes	76

VI. UNDERWORLD VIGNETTES

Underworld Vignette #1	82
Underworld Vignette #2	82
Underworld Vignette #3	83
Underworld Vignette #4	83
Underworld Vignette #5	84
Underworld Vignette #6	85
Underworld Vignette #7	85
Underworld Vignette #8	86

VII. WOMEN'S WORLD

J. Edgar Hoover's Seven Nastiest Women	88
Four Notorious Women Comment on Their Conviction	92
Five Shady Ladies	93

VIII. PRACTICAL ADVICE FOR THE FRIGHTENED

Seven Antimugger Rules	100
Six Facts You Should Know About Burglaries	101
Eight Ways to Burglarproof Your Home	102
Six Survival Tactics When You Find an Intruder in Your Home	103
Ten Ways to Burglarproof Your Home While on Vacation	104
Thirteen Breeds to Consider When Choosing a Watchdog	105
Thirteen Tips for the Woman Alone	108
Five Ways to Foil a Pickpocket	110

IX. IMPERFECT MURDERS: CRIMES THAT DIDN'T PAY

The Slightly Imperfect Murder #1: Seeds of Guilt	114
The Slightly Imperfect Murder #2: The Upside-Down Affair	116

The Slightly Imperfect Murder #3: The Impossible Dream House	117
The Slightly Imperfect Murder #4: Leftovers	119
The Slightly Imperfect Murder #5: The Plot Was All Wet	120
The Slightly Imperfect Murder #6: Losing One's Head	122
The Slightly Imperfect Murder #7: Sermon of Death	124
The Slightly Imperfect Murder #8: Garden of Evil	125
The Slightly Imperfect Murder #9: Spur of the Moment	127
The Slightly Imperfect Murder #10: Branded	128
The Slightly Imperfect Murder #11: Blood Will Tell	130
The Slightly Imperfect Murder #12: The Sit-Down Corpse	131
The Most Imperfect Murder #13: Clues, Clues, Clues	132

X. TRICKS, CONS, AND GYPS

Nine Con Games	136
Eight Carnival Gyps	139
Five Shortchanging Rackets	143
Six Communications from the COD Ghouls	146
Five Rules for Beating the Death Ghouls	148

XI. UNUSUAL WAYS TO AVOID DEATH AND OTHER PUNISHMENTS

Five Ways to Beat the Rap	150
Seven Incredible Escapes	152
Five Strange Ways to Avoid Execution	154
Seven Tough-to-Kill Victims	157
Six Bring-'Em-Back-Alive Cases	165

XII. CRIMES AND PEOPLE: THEY WORK IN MYSTERIOUS WAYS

Eight Crimes That Never Were	172
Comments by Eight Witnesses Who Didn't Help Kitty Genovese	176
Four "Postmortems"	178
Seven Strange Tales of Animals in the World of Crime	179
Ten Legal Rulings	182

Five Really Perfect Crimes

I.
MASTERS
OF THEIR TRADE

Seven Top Public Enemies

The 1930s were the heyday of the Public Enemy. Some who wore the label deserved the distinction. Others did not; their notoriety was the creation of a circulation-hungry press or authorities seeking to enhance their own reputations. Here are the seven best-known of the public enemies and their exploits.

1. John Dillinger. Beyond a doubt the greatest public enemy of all, John Dillinger raised the act of bank holdups to a fine art. All the Dillinger gang's robberies were meticulously planned. Even the least intelligent of the gang members was so trained that he knew his role perfectly and could react quickly even to unexpected developments. One police officer once said that Dillinger would have made a great football coach—or military general. Everything he did had style and verve. He escaped from jail on numerous occasions, once by brandishing a "pistol" he'd whittled out of wood. Dillinger was also a master at escaping from police traps, but his really great feats were his bank robberies.

The National Savings and Trust Company in Greencastle, Indiana, was in the center of a bustling community, with the courthouse and other government buildings clustered around it. It would be hard to take. Mr. Dillinger decided to go into the moviemaking business. The townspeople gathered in the streets to watch Dillinger's sidekick, Homer Van Meter, in action as a movie director. He sent Dillinger and Harry Pierpont to the bank entrance with machine guns while other members of the mob kept back the onlookers with the explanation "We're from Hollywood filming some bank-robbery scenes. Now, please keep back out of the way."

Phony cameras rolled and Dillinger and his sidekick charged forward and ran up the street. Van Meter was not pleased. "Let's do it again, only this time make the escape in the car and I want some people to run out of the bank yelling, 'It's a robbery,' and make it realistic." The boys went back—all the way into the bank.

It was most realistic. This time the boys came out with the loot from a very real robbery and piled into the car. All the technicians and the director also piled into the auto, then it sped off. That didn't seem to make much sense to the onlookers. By the time they discovered there had been a $74,000 real-life holdup, the robbers could have been well on their way to Hollywood.

The next day, Dillinger dropped a postcard to Matt Leach, his longtime police foe: "Did you see in the papers about that movie they made in Greencastle?"

On the night of July 2, 1934, after a young prostitute, Ann Sage, led him into a trap at the Biograph Theatre in Chicago, Dillinger was shot down by FBI agents. Or was he? The autopsy report, not made public for thirty years, revealed some strange contradictions. Dillinger's eyes had always been listed as blue; the dead man's were brown. Author Jay Robert Nash has made what appears to be a strong case that the man really killed was one Jimmy Lawrence, a small-time criminal, and that John Dillinger lived happily ever after.

2. Pretty Boy Floyd. Charles "Pretty Boy" Floyd was credited with being the first outlaw to use the machine gun extensively. At one time he even had a machine gun mounted on an automobile. He was labeled a twentieth-century Jesse James and he enjoyed the same popularity with large numbers of people that James had. Floyd was known as a hard worker who, unable to make a living, switched to robbing banks. He was an "Okie" and he had the respect of many other "Okies," especially in his war on banks. Floyd often tore up first mortgages when he robbed a banking institution, hoping that the mortgages had not been recorded.

All this gave him a sort of Robin Hood appeal—he tommy-gunned the rich for the benefit of the poor. His motives may be debated, but there is no doubt that he machine-gunned an awful lot of people. He was accused of being the machine gunner in the Kansas City Massacre, a charge he always denied even on his deathbed, after he was gunned down by FBI agents in Ohio in October 1934.

3. Baby Face Nelson. Lester Gillis was perhaps the maddest dog of the public enemies. Short, only five feet four and three-quarters inches tall, he had the face of a choirboy but the instincts of a killer shark. He killed for the slightest reason. He became furious when other gangs got the publicity for jobs he'd pulled. Finally, he joined the Dillinger gang and their jobs became bloodier affairs. Dillinger never felt comfortable with Baby Face Nelson around and soon they split up. After Dillinger's death Baby Face Nelson was happy when he at last found a prominent place on the FBI's wanted list. Nelson was finally cut down in a gun battle with two FBI agents near Barrington, Illinois. Nelson killed both agents but left the scene with seventeen bullets in various parts of his body. He died a short while later and his wife and a confederate dumped his nude body out of a car and onto a lonely road.

4. Alvin "Creepy" Karpis. Karpis became Public Enemy No. 1 after the death of John Dillinger, and is said to have been the gangster J. Edgar Hoover hated most. Karpis seemed to do the very things that inflamed Hoover. In 1935 Karpis held up a train, the first such robbery in years. He said he did it because it was a nostalgic touch, harking back to Jesse James, but mainly because he knew Hoover would consider it a personal affront. Hoover vowed to take Karpis personally, and when Karpis and another hoodlum were located in New Orleans, Hoover winged in to make the arrest. The capture was not the stuff dime novels were made of. After dozens of FBI agents closed in on Karpis and took him, there were some embarrassing moments when they realized that no one had brought along a pair of handcuffs. An agent's necktie was finally used. Then Karpis' captors tried to put leg shackles on him, but they couldn't get them to fit. In his memoirs Karpis maintained that Hoover was nowhere in sight when he was captured. He insists the FBI chief hid around the corner until other agents yelled to him that all was clear.

"He didn't lead the attack on me," Karpis states. "He hid until I was safely covered by many guns. He waited until he was told the coast was clear. Then he came out to reap the glory. . . . That May day in 1936, I made Hoover's reputation as a fearless lawman. It's a reputation he doesn't deserve."

5. Machine Gun Kelly. George Kelly makes the list of the Top Seven strictly by default, a bow to public opinion. All the evidence indicates that he was already out of his depth as a small-time bootlegger. Kathryn Kelly, his wife, made his reputation. She promoted him into something big in big-time crime. Yet Kelly did have a lasting impact. When he and Kathryn were cornered in their Memphis hideout, Kelly cowered in the far corner of a bedroom with his hands up and his heavy face twitching. "Don't shoot, G-men, don't shoot," he whimpered. He is famous for having given the FBI their popular name.

Kelly's lot in prison was not a happy one. His fellow convicts soon pegged him as something less than a public enemy and made him a butt of humor. Death in 1954 must have been a happy release for Machine Gun Kelly.

6. Clyde Barrow and Bonnie Parker. Among the public enemies, Bonnie and Clyde were really tiny-timers. The biggest job they ever pulled netted a mere $3,500, and that was *the* biggie. It was said Bonnie smoked cigars; she didn't, except for some gag photographs. They once kidnapped a police officer, and when Bonnie released him, she told him to tell the newspapers she didn't smoke cigars. He did, and Bonnie was very pleased.

If the pair were small-time robbers, they were big-time killers, having slain at least thirteen persons, many on whim. Yet, they spared others. There was a fierce loyalty among both Bonnie and Clyde and others who teamed with them from time to time. Both Pretty Boy Floyd and Baby Face Nelson ditched girls who were wounded, but Barrow never ditched Bonnie, defying incredible odds to come back and save her. In that sense, at least, they were the most heroic of the public enemies. They were killed in an ambush by a posse in May 1934. Twenty-five bullets were dug out of Clyde and twenty-three out of Bonnie.

7. Terrible Touhy. Roger "the Terrible" Touhy is another public enemy who doesn't belong on the list. He was the leader of the notorious Touhy gang—which didn't even exist. It was a hoax perpetrated by Touhy himself. Touhy was an independent trucker whose business did not prosper, so he shifted into trucking the most desired commodity of the time—bootleg whiskey. He locked up the liquor and beer business in Des Plaines, Illinois, and he grew quite prosperous as a result—so prosperous that Al Capone decided he wanted to control the action. He sent emissaries to Touhy to inform him of the decision. Touhy's response was to put on a show, one that sent Capone's emissaries back warning how tough the Touhy gang was. Touhy had merely borrowed pistols and machine guns, and staged a hoax. Buddies of his would parade in and out, muttering death threats. Touhy would order executions over the phone, making sure that the Capone men heard him. Capone drew back from a full-scale gang war against Terrible Touhy.

But finally the Capone organization got what it wanted by framing Touhy in a kidnapping case. Touhy served twenty-three years for a crime he didn't commit before a federal court released him with a scathing attack on the Capone mob, the Chicago police, the state's attorney, and the FBI. It also pointed out that Touhy had never been linked with a capital case, had never even made the public-enemies list of the Chicago Crime Commission. Touhy definitely did not deserve the label of public enemy. But someone did believe the label of Terrible Touhy. Twenty-three days after his release, Terrible Touhy was shot to death on a Chicago street.

The All-Time Ten Most-Wanted List of Murderers, Monsters, and Human Fiends

1. Elizabeth Bathory. Murders have been committed for bizarre reasons, by ghouls who wished to drink human blood or to inflict terrible horrors on helpless victims, but in all criminal history there seems to have been only one genuine blood-bath, that is, a real bath in human blood. That fantastic orgy was the work of a Hungarian countess named Elizabeth Bathory. The lady felt the urge for the grisly bath on New Year's Eve, 1610, and accordingly invited all the maidens from the area to her castle, Csethe. There a gala evening was enjoyed by all except the eight maidens who subsequently disappeared. They were bled to death to fill the countess' tub, in which she then bathed.

Exactly how the lady got into the nasty habit is probably best explained by experts Raymond T. McNally and Radu Florescu: "Elizabeth was afraid of becoming old and losing her beauty. One day a maid accidentally pulled her hair while combing it. Elizabeth instinctively slapped the girl, so hard that she drew blood, which spurted onto her own hand. It immediately seemed to Elizabeth as if her skin in this area took on the freshness of that of her young maid. Blood! Here was the key to an eternally beautiful skin texture. The countess then summoned Thorko and another accomplice, Johannes. They stripped the maid, cut her, and drained her blood into a huge vat. Elizabeth bathed in it to beautify her entire body."

Over the next ten years, Elizabeth murdered and tortured more than fifty girls; the culmination was the slaughter of eight girls at once. That was just too blatant and an investigation ensued. All of Elizabeth's accomplices were tried and executed. Elizabeth's fate was somewhat different. She was, after all, a countess. She was confined to her room. She died in 1614.

2. H. H. Holmes. (See also page 20). Herman W. Mudgett, or, as he is better known, Henry H. Holmes, was a bigamist, forger, swindler, horse thief, and murderer. His incredible "castle" in Chicago was loaded with secret stairways, trapdoors, soundproof rooms, torture chambers lined with sheet iron and asbestos, a crematory, vats of corrosive acid and quicklime, and gear with which he prepared skeletons for sale to medical schools. The actual number of persons he killed remains unknown. Two hundred is merely an educated guess. At least fifty visitors to the Chicago Fair of 1893 were traced to Holmes's door and never seen again. But Holmes, who once described himself as "an honest dealer in human remains," complicated the count by naming victims who turned up alive.

This caused the Chicago *Journal* to note rather indignantly: "The nerve, the calculation and the audacity of the man were unparalleled. Murder was his natural bent. Sometimes he killed from sheer greed of gain; oftener, as he has himself confessed, to gratify an inhuman thirst for blood. Not one of his crimes was the outcome of a sudden burst of fury—'hot blood'—as the codes say. All were deliberate;

planned and concluded with consummate skill. To him murder was indeed a fine art; and he reveled in the lurid glamour cast upon him by his abnormal genius. Even with the shadow of the noose dangling over his head, he evolved a so-called confession, detailing with horrible calmness how he had exterminated twenty-seven fellow creatures, and coldly setting forth the varied and bloody tortures he employed. One could almost see the fiendish grin on his thin and bloodless lips as, in the gloom of his cell, he set down the terrible tale. But the man was an atrocious liar, and several of these with whose murder he charged himself have since denied his story with their own lips. The statement was prompted by a perverted ambition to be regarded as the 'greatest' monster who ever walked in the form of man, and an incongruous desire to win for the education of his little son the $5,000 offered for the 'confession' by a newspaper."

Holmes didn't have to lie. He makes the list.

3. Sawney Beane and His Weird Tribe.

Today there is a much-traveled highway along the northwest coast of Great Britain that winds from Berwick-on-Tweed, at the Scottish border, up to Edinburgh, but in the 1600s this was no more than a straggling path. And on this path, over a period of twenty-five years, no fewer than 1,000 men, women, and children disappeared. All were the victims of Sawney Beane, a cannibal who lived with his wife in a cave just off the path. Beane would waylay passersby, kill them, then drag their bodies back to the cave. The victims' clothing would be saved, but their money and jewels were cast into the sea. The Beanes needed no money for food shopping. Over a quarter century the Beane clan expanded to fourteen sons and daughters and thirty-two grandchildren. As the clan grew the members hunted in a pack and could easily slay six horsemen in one foul swoop. Only half the travelers survived the journey from one end of the road to the other. The clan was caught and executed when the king realized he had to do something about it.

4. Murder Inc.'s Pittsburgh Phil.

Harry Strauss, alias Big Harry, alias Pep, alias Pittsburgh Phil, was the chief hit man for Murder Inc., the infamous killer squad from Brooklyn. New York authorities tied him to twenty-eight killings, and other law-enforcement agencies, from Connecticut to California, linked him to another twenty-eight. These are only the known ones. Most experts figure his total kill was between 100 and 200, give or take a few stiffs. Phil was also spontaneously savage. If he walked into a restaurant in Brownsville and by chance disliked a diner's face, he'd spit in his soup. If the patron uttered an objection, Phil would pick up the fork and slash the man's face with it. For this further breach of etiquette there was no redress. Those who ate in Brownsville generally lived there—but weren't eager to die suddenly there.

Phil was always upset when he wasn't around when the "troop" got an order and he got cut out of the action. When Phil killed, he did so with a touch of ghoulishness and, in a sense, a sort of poetry. Walter Sage was suspected of knocking down on the syndicate's slot machines. Phil killed him, lashed his body to a pinball machine, and tossed him in the drink. Symbols were important to Phil. He tried to kill one victim who was seated in the last row of a movie theater by getting the ax kept in a glass case in the event of fire. By the time he'd gotten the ax his intended victim had moved forward several rows. As Phil complained to the troop later, "Just when I get him set up, the bum turns out to be a goddamn chair-hopper."

5. Jane Toppan. She was an apple-cheeked, pink, plump, motherly type, and had the kind of face that could be used to advertise homemade jams. A nurse in Lowell, Massachusetts, at the turn of the last century, she had the reputation of being the area's most tender and capable healer of the sick. She was that and a bit more. "This is my ambition," she later told a horrified courtroom, "to have killed more people— more helpless people—than any man or any woman has ever killed." She is estimated to have turned more than a hundred sickbeds into deathbeds. She did it by concocting her own brand of poison, which fooled even the doctors. First she would build up her patient sufficiently so that the doctor would stop making regular calls. Then, slowly, she would begin poisoning the patient. First the patient's breathing would become short, painful gasps. Soon he would go into convulsions, then his body would relax, then become chilled, and again there would be convulsions and finally death.

"I can't quite describe the sensation," she declared at her trial. "I wanted to laugh. I would kiss the patient—simply because I was happy. I remember kissing Edith. I remember Edith still thought that I was trying to save her. If it hadn't been for her, I never would have been a nurse—and now I was paying her back."

"Paying her back, Miss Toppan?" Her own lawyer was shocked by his client. "What do you mean by 'paying her back'?"

"I don't know. She had been very kind to me."

Edith was Jane Toppan's stepsister.

Of course, Jane Toppan didn't kill all her patients. She did have her reputation to consider. One who survived her ministrations was Ellery Sedgwick, later the editor of *The Atlantic Monthly*. He was to write of Jane: "When it comes to evaluating the histories of famous murderers, Jane Toppan has never received proper recognition. Without the slightest doubt, she outranks both Bluebeard and Jack the Ripper."

Jane was finally caught and put away in an asylum for the rest of her life; thirty-one deaths attributed to her had been verified by the state, but only thirty-one bodies were exhumed. Other families refused to allow exhumation. They simply didn't want to know.

6. Hare and Burke. William Burke and William Hare were the inspirations for Robert Louis Stevenson's *The Body Snatchers*. In 1827 they started supplying bodies to Scottish medical schools. Nowadays medical schools have no trouble getting human cadavers for dissection and study. At first Scottish law allowed a bona fide school only "one malefactor's body a year" for experimentation. Later this was increased to include the bodies of a few more suicides and criminals. This quota went to the official university school in Edinburgh only, and rival schools of medicine got no bodies. Thus was born the trade of body snatching in Scotland. Many students raided graves to get material for their homework, and bands of professional grave robbers sprang up. Hare and Burke revolutionized the trade. It was very troublesome, even dangerous, to raid graves. They decided to make their own corpses and did so with great efficiency. One such victim was Mary Haldame, whom they got drunk on rum and then strangled. A week later, her daughter Kathy came looking for her. Hare and Burke could do nothing but finish her off as well and ship the body over to Surgeon's Square.

When they were caught, Hare testified against Burke at a trial that became a worldwide sensation. Sir Walter Scott was in the courtroom as a reporter. Burke was hanged and the reputation of Dr. Robert Knox, their chief buyer for his anatomy school, was ruined. When Hare was set free, angry crowds pursued him but he finally escaped. Over the next two weeks, dozens of men were beaten in various parts of Scotland because they were mistaken for Hare. The verb "to burke" comes from William Burke and means to kill by suffocation with few or no signs of violence.

7. Albert Fish. Readers with tender stomachs should move on immediately to number 8. Fish was an elderly, almost angelic-looking house painter in New York City who killed and ate at least seventeen children, generally after making them into a stew with carrots and onions. Fish was sentenced to death, but hardly looked on his punishment as punishment. It was the greatest thrill of his life. He even helped them adjust the electrodes when he was strapped into the electric chair on January 16, 1936.

8. Fritz Haarmann. Readers who skipped number 7 should move directly to number 9. Fritz Haarmann attempted to solve Germany's World War I famine single-handedly by murdering approximately fifty boys and young men in Hanover. He dismembered the bodies and converted the meat into sausages. When he was caught and brought to trial in 1924, the sale of sausages in Germany dropped tremendously. Found guilty, Haarmann was decapitated.

9. Joseph Briggen's Hungry Brood. Joseph Briggen lived his fifty-odd years in a remote California valley without ever arousing suspicion. Folks knew Briggen didn't make much of a living on his Sierra Morena Ranch. He never needed more than one hired hand at a time. But people knew Briggen had other things to make him happy, for example, his prize Berkshire swine. Every fall he would enter his beloved animals in the state fair at Sacramento. Folks couldn't remember when he had not won the coveted blue ribbon in that category. During these days Briggen was in his glory, and when visitors would ask him about the care and feeding of his animals, Briggen's ordinarily stern face would crack into a broad smile. He'd explain that the beasts were all he had and that he treated them as if they were little children. But these moments of glory drew a terrible price. Briggen would hire homeless men as his hired hands, and when, after some weeks, they would demand their back pay, he would kill them, chop them up—and feed them to his prize swine. Briggen was convinced it was this diet that made his swine prizewinners. When he was caught, authorities dug up the bones of at least twelve different men, and they hadn't even located all the hiding places. Briggen was sent to San Quentin for life in 1902, and died shortly thereafter. Someone said he died of a broken heart at having to miss the fair.

10. Billy Gohl. Next to H. H. Holmes, Billy Gohl was one of the most mechanized of murderers. He was a walking delegate of the Sailors' Union of the Pacific in Aberdeen, Washington, and when sailors got to town, they'd check with Gohl for mail and leave their valuables with him. Union delegates always kept money in the safe until the sailors called for it. Not Billy Gohl. He just kept it. When a new sailor came in, Billy would look out the window to see if anybody was around. If there wasn't, he'd take the man's money, pull a gun out of a desk drawer, and shoot the unsuspecting man in the head. He'd clean his gun and put it away, search the sailor's body for additional money, and then get rid of the body. Gohl's office was on the second floor of a building the back of which extended out over the Wishkah River, which flowed into Gray's Harbor. Supported by stilts, the house had a trapdoor in the floor with a chute leading down to the water. The body would go down the chute and into the river. The fast current would carry a body away immediately. It would be days or weeks, if at all, before the body would float to the surface many miles away.

After 1903, when Billy Gohl first came to Aberdeen, the seamen started calling the town "the Port of Missing Men." Between 1909 and 1912 a total of forty-one "floaters" were fished out of Gray's Harbor. Almost all of them were merchant seamen. The most indignant man was Billy Gohl. He demanded the town's police do something. Finally the law put two and two together and did just that. Gohl beat execution only because the state of Washington had just eliminated capital punishment. He got life and died in 1928.

Four Back-up Murderers, Monsters, and Human Fiends from the California "Little League"

In compiling any most-wanted list of mass murderers the tendency is to think in worldwide terms, but there's a "Little League" in California in which all the backups that could possibly be needed can be found. Here are four recent candidates who just don't make the international top ten—but through no fault of their own.

1. Herbert Mullin. Right after Kemper's murder splurge, another Californian, Herbert Mullin, aged twenty-six, a college dropout and junkie, went on a three-week tear, killing ten persons. Mullin's attorney claimed he would show that his client, once voted by his high-school classmates as most likely to succeed, was stark, raving mad. Mullin claimed he was telepathically instructed to kill. He also believed that California was in imminent danger of sliding into the Pacific Ocean and only his offering of human sacrifices could prevent it. When asked why he killed his victims, Mullin responded, "They didn't want me to relate. . . . I'm a scapegoat person made to carry the guilt feelings of others. . . . Every day people die. There's a steady flow of death in order to keep the coast free of cataclysmic earthquakes and the earth in orbit." Mullin was sentenced to life imprisonment for the ten murders. He was not tried for three others he had confessed to, including the stomping-and-stabbing murder of a Roman Catholic priest in Los Gatos, California, after he'd listened to Mullins' confession.

2. The Zodiac Killer. California can be counted on regularly to produce a wholesale murderer of females. In 1978 an unknown murderer apparently killed a dozen-odd girls. It was still conjecture then if all the murders were the work of the same person, but now there is no doubt that there is only one so-called Zodiac Killer. Sheriff Don Streipeke, of Sonoma County, California, was the first law officer to expound the lone-killer theory in the slaying of thirty or more young women in five Western states, including at least fourteen women in California, between December 1969 and December 1973. The Zodiac Killer taunted authorities with messages claiming his thirty-seven victims were destined to be his slaves in an afterlife. Six girls he killed in the Santa Rosa area were heaved great distances over a bank near running water. All the girls had their hair parted in the middle and had pierced ears. Near some of the victims was a zodiac sign related to English witchcraft. This witchcraft sign would be placed on the hearth of an English home after a death had occurred so that the deceased would be sped along to the afterlife. All the girls had been hitchhiking when they disappeared, all were found nude, and their clothing and belongings were never located. The Zodiac killings remain unsolved.

3. Charles Manson. On August 9, 1969, a man, Charles "Tex" Watson, and three girls, Susan Atkins, Leslie Van Houten, and Patricia Krenwinkel, entered the Roman Polanski estate in Beverly Hills and murdered actress Sharon Tate, eight months pregnant, and four others. Two nights later, the same foursome broke into the home of Leno and Rosemary La Bianca, brutally killed them, and used their blood to scrawl messages on the wall. The murderers were soon traced back to a "family" headed by Charles Manson, at thirty-four a "graduate" of several prisons and reform schools. The Manson Family indulged in free love and drug bouts, and practiced guerrilla tactics. When Manson commanded, they also practiced murder. All—including Manson, the mass murderer by proxy—were given the death sentence. When the U.S. Supreme Court voided such sentences, they were given life imprisonment. All have been eligible for parole since 1978, but have been denied it up until now.

4. Juan Corona. One of the more prolific murderers in California history, Juan Corona was convicted of killing twenty-five migrant farm workers in 1970 and 1971. The case against Corona was overwhelming. As a murderer he had the finesse of a gored bull. He buried his victims in shallow graves in the peach orchards of Yuba City, forty-five miles north of Sacramento. Unfortunately for him, some receipts belonging to Corona were found in one grave and some of his bank-deposit slips in another. When authorities got around to searching Corona's home, they found bloodstained objects and clothing all over the place. Among them were two butcher's knives, a machete, a pistol, a Levi jacket, and some shorts. Corona was often seen washing out the inside of his van, a convenient vehicle for transporting corpses to the peach orchards.

Corona, exhibited unusually good graces in court. After the verdict he asked his lawyer to thank the jury for its "patience."

The Corona case did not end with the convicted man's being sentenced to twenty-five consecutive life terms. In 1978 three District Court of Appeals judges ordered a new trial because, they said, his lawyer had failed to represent him properly by not even trying for an "obvious" insanity plea. In a seventy-one-page opinion reversing the conviction, the lawyer, Richard Hawk, was described as serving "two masters with conflicting interests." One was Corona's right to fair representation; the other, attorney Hawk's own wallet. To pay Hawk's fee, Corona had given him the exclusive rights to the story. The lawyer got a book contract, and from that point on, the judges believed, his intention was to make the Corona story more interesting, apparently by making it all the more mysterious. Not, mind you, that the judges doubted the verdict. The weight of the evidence against Corona was conclusive, but he was still entitled to a new trial. The next step in the case was a mental-competency hearing—with the likelihood, according to many observers, that Corona had served his last day behind prison walls.

The Three Greatest Swindlers

The fine art of flimflam and swindling requires great skill, and it is difficult to choose the top three artists. There was, for example, Arturo Alves Reis, who conned the London firm of Waterlow & Sons, which printed bank notes for the Bank of Portugal, into issuing $10 milion worth of 500- and 1,000-escudo notes directly to him. In this unusual arrangement Reis had presented forged letters of approval, allegedly from the Bank of Portugal's governor. With this money Reis started his own private bank in Lisbon and then began buying up shares of the Bank of Portugal with the idea of becoming its major stockholder and in time getting full control. This would have meant that, in effect, he would have owned Portugal. He was fouled by a duplication of serial numbers and went to prison for fifteen years; released in 1945, he died broke ten years later.

There was also George C. Parker, who died in Sing Sing in 1937 at the age of seventy-six. This swindler can be said to have sold New York City hundreds of times over. During a career that lasted forty-five years, Parker sold to gullible out-of-towners such prize structures as the Brooklyn Bridge, Madison Square Garden, Grant's Tomb, the Statue of Liberty, and the Metropolitan Museum of Art. The Brooklyn Bridge was sold twice a month for sums up to $50,000. When a poor sucker didn't have enough money to pay for it, Parker would very understandingly take a down payment and the balance in installments. Naturally, the victim could not take possession until full payment was received. But these are only the pikers. The champion swindlers follow.

1. Charles A Ponzi. The greatest swindler ever to operate in the United States was Charles Ponzi, an Italian who came to America in 1899 and worked at odd jobs, such as dishwashing. He had, however, a very agile mind and actually did come up with a genuine money-making gimmick. He found that it was possible to buy up international postal-union–reply coupons at depressed prices in, say, France and to sell them in the United States for close to a 50-percent profit. That was not a bad get-rich-slowly strategy, but Ponzi then found a quicker and better variation on the theme. He told people exactly what he was doing and said he needed a lot of capital to make a lot of money. For the use of their money Ponzi promised people a 50-percent return in three months. That was a difficult offer to refuse, and the money rolled in to Ponzi's Boston office. Pretty soon he had to open offices in nearby states.

The money continued to pour in, especially when he actually started sending out his first interest payments. On one day alone Ponzi's offices took in $2 million—and that was in 1920 dollars. His clerks couldn't handle the deluge and incoming cash had to be stuffed in desk drawers, closets, and even wastebaskets under the counter. The more that came in, the more Ponzi paid out. In fact, that was the whole key to Ponzi's scheme. He was using the fresh money to pay the interest on the old money. As long as the flow didn't slow up, he was all right. When the newspapers started getting suspicious and began to investigate, he promptly hit them with a half-million-dollar lawsuit that kept the lid on for a while. Meanwhile, Ponzi was living high on the hog. He collected a wardrobe of more than 200 suits, had no fewer than two dozen diamond stickpins, and bought himself a huge mansion. When the bubble finally burst, it was found that Ponzi had taken in something like $20 million and had paid out about half. The other half couldn't be accounted for. Ponzi was clapped into jail twice for his monumental fraud and later deported to Italy.

This should have been the end of the story but the facts are that Mussolini greeted the great "financial genius" with open arms. Exactly what happened next was blurred by Fascist censorship, but eventually Ponzi found it wise to leave Italy. The rumor was that the Italian treasury had suffered something similar to the Boston version of the "lights." For a while Ponzi worked for an Italian company in Rio de Janeiro, a position he held until 1939. Then he went downhill; all his money was gone, he was partially blind and paralyzed, and he ended up in the charity ward of a hospital in Rio. He died in January 1949.

2. Serge Alexander Stavisky. Stavisky was a Ukrainian with a long record of business fraud and swindling who nonetheless maneuvered himself into control of the public finances of the city of Bayonne, France. In the process he made millions for himself, but his grand thefts would have been impossible without the assistance of large numbers of influential and corrupt government officials. With so many people involved, leaks developed, and Stavisky's grand scheme for milking France collapsed. Stavisky shot himself. A government crisis ensued, with the political Left and Right each accusing the other of having been involved in Stavisky's dealings. Twenty defendants were indicted, and scores of others kept insisting they were not involved. Even Madame Arlette Stavisky, widow of the archswindler, was indicted. One of the magistrates investigating the affair was found dead on the railroad tracks near Dijon.

The investigation was a Gallic shambles, and in the end the French public really had no idea of who had, or had not, done what. The public treasury was, however, considerably poorer. In 1936 Madame Stavisky was acquitted. She got a number of offers of marriage and for stage, radio, and film engagements. She accepted an eight-week stint in a New York nightclub.

3. Ivar Kreuger, the Swedish Match King. Kreuger built the greatest financial empire of all time, theoretically on matches. He eventually controlled the supply of two-thirds of all matches in the world, as well as scores of other businesses—mines, newspapers, banks, and telephone companies. He had holding companies built upon holding companies, and no one else in his organization knew much about his operations. Whenever Kreuger needed a few tens of millions of dollars, he would issue a glowing financial report on one company, extolling its holdings in some unprofitable and sometimes even nonexistent companies. Investors, including large banks, fought to buy some of the securities. Kreuger became known as the financial savior of the world as he made huge loans to more than a dozen countries, including Spain, Poland, Greece, Hungary, Yugoslavia, and France. In exchange for these loans, Kreuger won monopolistic control of that country's match industry.

With that control he raised additional bank credits and started the whole cycle over again, buying up another railroad or forest or gold mine or telephone company. International bankers and political leaders came to him hat in hand. A top banker might be sitting at Kreuger's desk when his phone would ring and Kreuger would speak with Mussolini of Italy. The Match King would promptly scream at Il Duce that he was not keeping his nation's finances in proper shape. The banker would leave Kreuger properly impressed. After Kreuger's death it was discovered that he had a hidden button under his desk with which he rang his phone when he wished to stage a performance. Mussolini never had called him, but the impressed banker told only his banking associates, and so the Kreuger hoax grew.

Kreuger's downfall, like that of so many others, came in the crash of 1929. He could not raise more money. Investors tried to sell their holdings in his firms, but there was no longer any way for Kreuger to pay them off. On March 12, 1932, at the age of fifty-two, the fabulous Match King shot himself. It took years to try to straighten out his bizarre, nonexistent financial empire. When dozens of investigators finally completed their study, they found that Kreuger had skimmed off at least $500 million for his personal use. He had maintained five homes in as many cities and three country estates. His personal weekly spending money was $180,000.

Four Recent "Loner" Assassins and Their Strange "Inferiority"

Magazine writer Jack Stewart was the first to note the weird coincidence involved in the four most shocking assassinations, attempted or completed, in recent American history. According to Stewart, ours is a tradition remarkably strong in assassinations. In many cases the assassin has a shorter name than his victim's—Lincoln-Booth, Rasputin-Yusupov, for example. Stewart theorizes that the very fact that a potential assassin has a shorter name than his victim's is a contributing motive for the crime. In America's four most recent and significant assassination attempts the coincidence is even more pronounced. The assassin in each case had a name one letter shorter than his victim's.

1. John F. Kennedy (seven) by Lee Harvey Oswald (six).
2. Martin Luther King, Jr. (four), by James Earl Ray (three).
3. Robert F. Kennedy (seven) by Sirhan Sirhan (six).
4. George C. Wallace (seven) by Arthur H. Bremer (six).

Stewart dismisses the fact that Gerald Ford was twice the victim of an attempted assassination by women with longer names than his—Lynette Alice Fromme and Sara Jane Moore. In an observation that may bring down the wrath of feminists, Stewart observes that women seem to be laboring under the weight of other "inferiorities."

Eight Infamous Lady Killers

1. H. H. Holmes. Herman W. Mudgett, Holmes's real name, was without question America's greatest criminal. He murdered perhaps 200 women for their money and squeezed every cent out of his murders. In his cellar he kept a complete supply of surgical instruments and operating tables, and when he spotted an ad in the paper for a skeleton, he would scrape a victim's skeleton clean and sell it to a medical institution.

Holmes in 1892 built a massive "hotel"—really a murder factory—at Sixty-third and Wallace in Chicago. The first story was given over to stores, and there were about 100 rooms on the second and third floors. Holmes maintained his own living quarters and an office there; the rest of the rooms were for "guests." Many rooms were really cells and others were execution chambers.

One room was to be labeled later by a newspaper as an "asphyxiation chamber—no light—with gas connections." This room was windowless, the door was equipped with stout bolts, and the walls were lined with asbestos. Holmes would lock a victim in this room and turn on the gas. Almost all the rooms had gas connections; some had false floors that covered small, airless chambers; some were lined with iron plates and some came with wicked-looking blowtorchlike appliances. There were several chutes down which corpses could be dropped to the basement. Holmes had a trapdoor in the floor of his bathroom on the second floor that led down to a small cubicle between-floors. Here, too, there was a slick chute leading to the cellar. In the cellar were a crematory, quicklime pits, and vats of corrosive acid for the efficient disposal of bodies. In the pits below the cellar were found fragments of skulls and bones of the many women he had tricked and killed. All the second-floor rooms were rigged to an alarm system that rang a buzzer in Holmes's quarters, warning him if any of his prisoners were trying to escape. Apparently some of the women were held prisoner for months before he got around to disposing of them.

Holmes lured some of his victims with the promise of marriage and others with the promise of a good job in the big city. Most of his victims either lived alone or had no close relatives. He induced them to bring their life savings with them. Those who didn't were apparently induced to reveal the whereabouts of their wealth when placed in various kinds of apparatus that were similar to medieval torture racks, also found later in the basement. It is also likely that some victims were used in experiments to prove Holmes's pet theory that the human body is capable of being stretched indefinitely, a biological "fact" that would lead eventually to the development of a race of giants. Oddly enough, Holmes was able to keep up his evil enterprise for four years without arousing suspicion. Ironically, he was eventually arrested for killing a man in Philadelphia, in an insurance swindle, and Chicago police searched his "hotel"—with astonishing results. Holmes was hanged on May 7, 1896.

2. Henri Landru. In a manner of speaking, it is the rankest sort of injustice that Landru, or Bluebeard, is remembered as the king of lady killers instead of Holmes. True, Landru loved 283 women—but Holmes killed almost that many. Landru killed only ten women. But Landru must be given his due; he had Gallic charm and wit. He was an artist, Holmes a mere technician. Charlie Chaplin played the former type in *Monsieur Verdoux*. Landru selected his victims only after careful screening. His notebook showed that he carefully classified all replies to his matrimonial advertisements and filled out information on each woman's fortune, children, and relatives. The women were listed under the following categories:

1. To be answered *poste restante*.
2. Without money.
3. Without furniture.
4. No reply.
5. To be answered to initials *poste restante*.
6. Possible fortune.
7. To be further investigated.

Landru kept careful accounts on all his expenditures so that the exact profit could be determined after each lady was dispatched. Perhaps Landru saw the grim humor in all of this. He did see the black humor of his trial. He maintained his innocence and was silent even as indisputable evidence piled up against him. He was amused by the women who flocked to the trial and he seemed to be still on the make. When one woman could not find a seat in the gallery, he offered her his in the dock. Remarkably, after finding him guilty of ten murders, the jury nonetheless recommended mercy for him. The judge turned them down, and Landru was guillotined on February 23, 1922.

3. John George Haigh. The sensational British press dubbed him "The Vampire Killer" after Haigh confessed to six murders and claimed that after each killing he had drunk the victim's blood. This may or may not have been true, but his confession was made in the hope of sustaining an insanity plea.

Haigh's downfall came after the murder of sixty-nine-year-old Mrs. Henrietta Helen Olivia Robarts Durand-Deacon. Haigh had invited her to visit his "factory" at Crawley in Sussex. Mrs. Durand-Deacon had a £40,000 legacy but kept herself busy with various business ventures. She'd been working on designs for artificial fingernails that she hoped could be manufactured in plastic. Haigh drove her out to an isolated factory where they could work on the matter—and he was ready for her. As soon as they got inside he shot her through the nape of the neck. He stripped the widow's body of a Persian-lamb coat, necklace, earrings, rings, and crucifix. Then he stuck the body in an anticorrosive drum, poured in sulfuric acid, and worked it around with a stirrup pump. When the acid had completed its job, Haigh left and popped in at Ye Olde Ancient Priors Restaurant for a spot of tea and poached eggs on toast. Eventually, however, the police learned that Haigh was the last one to see the widow and he confessed with a superior air. He admitted to the killing but reminded the police that they had no body. The police did find just enough bone and tooth fragments to identify the victim. Trapped at last, Haigh went into his vampire act. It laid an egg with the jury, and he was hanged on August, 10, 1949.

4. Joe Ball. The Sociable Inn in Elmendorf, Texas, run by a former bootlegger, Joe Ball, was famous for two things. The waitresses were all incredibly lovely and the alligators kept in a pond out in back were incredibly mean and ugly. The big attraction was the 'gators' feeding time. Ball would gather up stray dogs and cats, and feed them live to the awful reptiles. Those customers who were too squeamish could just stay inside and watch the waitresses. They often had to watch fast. One day a waitress might be there and the next day she would be gone. When asked about that, Ball would say, "They come, they go." The trouble was that some would go, leaving their belongings behind.

When the family of Minnie Mae Gotthardt wrote to complain that they hadn't heard from her for some time, the police dropped in on Ball, who told them she'd left for a new job. They left satisfied. A few months later, they were back asking about Julia Turner, another waitress. He told the same story. Well, what about the fact that she'd left all her belongings behind with her roommate? Ball explained he was a pushover for the ladies; he'd given her $500 for her bus fare to California and enough for a new wardrobe, and she'd left. The law was satisfied again. But when two more waitresses disappeared, the Texas Rangers got involved. They had a whole list of waitresses who'd disappeared. This time Ball couldn't think of a good story, so he stepped behind the bar, pulled out a gun, and shot himself.

Later, the Rangers found a batch of letters in Ball's effects that indicated that eight waitresses who'd left the job were coming back to Ball because he'd made them pregnant. None could be found. The law questioned an old man who had worked for Ball and he finally confessed that Ball had killed most of the girls and fed them to his pet alligators. The man said he'd been forced to help under threat of death. The story was confirmed by a rancher who'd left Elmendorf two years earlier, in 1936. One night some cattle of his had broken out of his pasture and he set out to round them up. He rode up behind Ball's roadhouse and came on Ball butchering the body of a girl and tossing the pieces to his alligators. When Ball spotted the rancher, he pulled a gun and forced him to dismount. When Ball told the man he'd have to kill him, the rancher begged for his life and vowed to say nothing. Ball finally relented because the rancher had a large family. He gave the rancher $500 and told him to get out of the county in twenty-four hours. The man fled to California with his family the next day, later selling his ranch through a broker. He had feared to return to Elmendorf until he read that Ball was dead.

5. George Joseph Smith. A notorious bigamist, Smith became famous as England's "Brides in the Bath" murderer. He preyed on lonely women, married them, insured them—and drowned them in the bathtub. Smith was a stickler about this. He took one of his brides, Bessie Mundy, to live in lodgings that, he was shocked to find, had no bathtub. The next day, he bought one secondhand, carried it home, and installed it himself. Eleven days later, Bessie was found dead in the tub. The official verdict was that she'd had an epileptic seizure and drowned. Finally, under the name of Lloyd, Smith married Margaret Lofty. She, too, drowned in the bath. This sad death occurred on a Friday evening and attracted the attention of the weekend press. The following Sunday, the *News of the World* ran a tearjerker with the headline BRIDE'S TRAGIC FATE ON DAY AFTER WEDDING. The families of several other brides who'd met similar fates read the story and went to the police even though their daughters had not been married to a Mr. Lloyd. Mr. Lloyd was found to be Mr. Smith and Mr. Smith was hanged in 1915.

6. John Reginald Christie. Almost all mass murderers of women, such as the preceding five, are swindlers who graduate to lady-killing. Others, however, are sexually driven. John Reginald Christie had strong sexual habits. It appears he could engage in the sex act only with partners who were unconscious. He made them unconscious in an unusual way. In 1939 Christie either tricked or forced Ruth Fuerst into inhaling gas, and then he raped and killed her. Since his wife was due home shortly, Christie hid the girl's body under the living-room floorboards of his London apartment until he could get around to burying her in the garden. Next, Christie gave the same treatment to a friend of his wife, Muriel Eady. By that time Christie decided he couldn't very well hide corpses around the house where his wife could find them—so he killed his wife. In the first three months of 1953 Christie killed three more women. Then Christie moved out of his flat. The next tenant found three bodies in a hidden cupboard and called the police, who found three more bodies in the garden and under the floorboards. On July 15, 1953, Christie, the corpse saver, was hanged.

7. The Boston Strangler. For three years, beginning in 1963, one woman after another was found sexually molested and strangled in the Boston area. It was not until after the thirteenth victim was found that the murderous reign of terror of the Boston Strangler ended with the confession of Albert H. DeSalvo.

DeSalvo, a thirty-four-year-old mental patient, had a long record of sexually perverse crimes. There was no doubt that DeSalvo was the Strangler. He could relate scores of details that only the murderer could have known. His attorney, F. Lee Bailey, made a convincing argument for committing him to a mental hospital for life. But there were others who considered DeSalvo crazy . . . crazy like a fox. One reporter spent thirty days in a cell in Walpole State Prison with DeSalvo as a neighbor and relates that DeSalvo reveled in the stares he got in the visitor's room. "Look at them looking at me," he was quoted as having said. "They're asking the guy who they are visiting, 'Is that the Boston Strangler?' Ha, they even know me in the Soviet Union." DeSalvo's favorite pastime: inscribing a paperback book by Gerold Frank about him and then passing it to female visitors through the bars. The inscription reads, "Can't wait to get my hands around your throat."

8. Richard Speck. In July 1966 Richard Speck stunned America with the savage murders of eight student nurses in the living quarters of the South Chicago Community Hospital. A ninth nurse, Corazon Amurao, managed to hide under a bed, and was overlooked by Speck as he killed his victims one by one. After he left she ran screaming from the apartment and was able to provide police with a description of the killer. Later, Speck attempted to cut his wrists in his room in a ninety-cents-a-day Chicago skid-row flophouse, and was identified when brought to the hospital for treatment. He was quickly convicted of the crime and a jury recommended the electric chair. In 1971, however, the state supreme court threw out the death penalty, and Speck was given eight consecutive sentences of 50 to 150 years. Since that time Speck has managed to keep himself in the limelight with several obviously futile bids for parole and with other "confessions." In 1978 he announced that he had not committed the murders alone but had had two accomplices. What had become of them? Speck said he was sure they would have turned him in, so he "had to kill them, too."

The Three Most Audacious Crime Plots

1. Operation America. Without a doubt the most incredible and daring plot to plunder and destroy many American cities at the same time was originated and orchestrated by a master criminal, John A. Murrel, in the 1830s. Operating out of his Arkansas headquarters, Murrel used his extensive criminal connections to recruit a strike force of 5,000 outlaws, killers, thieves, and swindlers who were to swoop down on various cities on "rebellion day." To further aid his plan, he sent agents into the South to incite the slaves to revolt at the same time. This unrest would preoccupy civil authorities and on Christmas Day, 1835, Murrel's gangs would strike out on their rob-and-destroy attacks. Murrel's plan called for setting ablaze such cities as New Orleans, Vicksburg, Mobile, and Memphis, as well as a host of smaller ones. Then the plunderers would rob banks and seize jewelry, gold, silver, and other valuables. By hitting so many cities at once, Murrel hoped to so confuse federal authorities that they would not know how to respond in time. But the plan was so grandiose that by its nature many persons had to know of it in advance. Government agents learned about it and with lightning raids were able crush it before it got rolling.

2. The Great Underworld Raid. The French underworld has always been considered the most daring, resourceful, and cunning in the world, and nowhere is that fact better demonstrated than in its "great pardoning act of 1944." Many of France's national criminal records were kept in Marseilles, and with World War II raging, the underworld saw their golden opportunity. In a mass attack, gangsters broke into police headquarters and stole all the criminal records. This could have happened only in Marseilles, the most lawless city in the Western world. In fact, a prewar survey had shown that of all major crimes committed in all of France from 1900 to 1930, 75 percent had been by persons who were born or who lived in this Mediterranean seaport.

3. The Robbery of the British Crown Jewels. Visitors today to the Tower of London see the crown jewels and are regaled with the tale of Colonel Thomas Blood, a common ruffian who almost stole them. In 1671 Blood and two confederates dressed as clergymen gained entrance to the tower and were given permission to see the crown jewels. Then Blood pulled a mallet from under his coat and slugged the custodian. The trio tried to file the big scepter in half but had to abandon the effort. The trio took off with the orb and the ceremonial crown. They almost made it, but were caught at the outer gate of the tower. Yet, surprisingly, Blood and his accomplices were not executed. King Charles II was so taken by the sheer gall of the plot that he granted all three a royal pardon and gave Blood a position at court. That, at least, is the official line, but later it was suspected that Blood sold the king on a plot, a plot that would provide the free-spending "Merry Monarch" with a huge amount of money. None of that was absolutely proved but history does show that when King Charles died, in 1685, shocked officials discovered a sad fact about the coronation crown. All the precious jewels had been removed and replaced with worthless imitations. For years thereafter, former mistresses of the late king kept turning up with a crown jewel or two. The stealing of the crown jewels was a daring plot, fully worthy of a rogue like Blood—or of a playboy king.

Hunting for the Forty Notches on Wes Hardin's Gun

A mystique has grown about the number of victims of such men as Jesse James, Billy the Kid, and Butch Cassidy—the most famous gunmen and outlaws of the Old West. The answer is a mere handful or two. Only one outlaw really killed on a wholesale basis and could fill his gun with notches. He was Wes Hardin, who had, according to legend, forty notches. This may be a bit of an exaggeration but not much. Looking at the findings of a number of Western researchers, let's see if Hardin is entitled to his forty—count 'em—reputation.

Wes, a circuit-riding preacher's son, started his killing days in 1868, when Texas was undergoing Reconstruction. Wes was fifteen and too young to have done any fighting in the war and kill himself some damn Yankees and now they were all over the place, together with numerous newly freed blacks. The latter took their new citizenship too seriously for Wes, so he shot one (1).

Wes was surprised that the damn Yankee soldiers took that so seriously. When three soldiers came after him, he gunned them all down (2, 3, 4). Wes drifted on to new parts and, having turned sixteen, popped off another soldier (5) after some slight disagreement. At this tender age Wes Hardin took to playing cards for money and got into a game with a well-known desperado named Bradley, who had drifted down to Texas from up north. A dispute developed over whether a flush beat a straight or some such, and Bradley settled the matter by pulling his gun and shooting the table. He couldn't do any better because in the meantime Wes had shot him squarely between the eyes (6).

Then along came a big, tough canvasman with the John Robinson circus who'd heard tales around Horn Hill about Hardin's pistol prowess and said they were nonsense. The trouble was that he said it to Hardin's face and the circus had to bury a canvasman (7). Over in Kosse, Texas, a city slicker cornered innocent Wes in the badger game. He told Wes he'd have to make things right. Wes did—right between the eyes (8).

Then Wes killed a barber named Huffman (9), a shooting he always denied—perhaps because a deputy named Jim Smolly arrested him for the killing and started taking him to Waco to face charges. There's no denying what happened to Deputy Smolly on the way (10).

After that Wes went home to visit his pa, who allowed it might be a good idea if his son lit out for Mexico. Wes headed for the border but was captured by three Texas state policemen. Wes didn't stay caught long (11, 12, 13). He continued on to Gonzales, which was as close as he got to Mexico. A Mexican monte dealer was not about to take guff from a little gringo like Wes, at least that was what he said (14).

By this time Wes was close to seventeen years old. He decided to head north for Kansas. Along the way, he killed an Indian (15), then another Indian, who was trying to steal some cattle (16). Wes took umbrage at some sorts of lawbreaking.

Then a Mexican trail boss didn't like the names Hardin called him, grabbed a rifle and fired at Hardin at a distance. He grazed Hardin's hat but then did a really stupid thing. He hopped on his horse and rode straight at Wes to gun him down. Not too many men ever rode straight at Hardin's .45 Colt (17). The other Mexicans in the outfit tried to take Wes on. He plugged four of them (18, 19, 20, 21).

Wes reached Abilene, where Wild Bill Hickok was marshal, and promptly shot a man named Brewster or Brewer or some such (22). Not wanting to have to explain things to Hickok, he took off for Cottonwood, where a cowboy named Bill Coran had been slain by some Mexican. Wes promptly shot the Mexican (23), which made him popular with the cowboys, and he went back to Abilene. Hickok just nodded approvingly at him. Hardin's next killing really was in self-defense. He'd had a good night at the gaming tables and had retired to his room when a sneak thief tried to kill him in his sleep. Wes awoke to find a knife poised above him. He always slept with his Colt and fired. The thief crawled into the hallway and died (24). By this time killing seemed to be predictable around Wes in Abilene and he got out before Hickok and his men could corral him.

He caught three members of a posse Hickok sent after him but let them live, sending them homeward without pants. Then two black policemen found him in a small-town grocery store. Wes had his back to the door and one policeman covered him while the other waited outside. Wes held out his Colt, handle first, toward his captor, but his finger was hooked in the trigger guard. As the lawman reached for the weapon Wes executed the "road agent's spin" and shot him dead (25). The other policeman fled.

Another posse came after Wes shortly after that but he discouraged the chase by killing three of them (26, 27, 28).

Then, along the road to Gonzales, a Mexican highwayman accosted Wes. "Reach!" he ordered. Wes reached for his gun (29). Then, in Willis, three lawmen who didn't know Hardin accosted him: "Some fellows tried to arrest me for carrying a pistol. They got the contents of it instead" (30, 31, 32).

By that time warrants for Hardin papered Texas. Shortly thereafter, he was wounded in a gun battle and was lying in bed when two officers stumbled upon his hideout. From his bed Wes shot one (33) and wounded the other. Wes staggered off, but he decided the best thing he could do was surrender, so he sent word to a lawman he trusted, Sheriff Dick Reagan. He was jailed in Austin, and when his wounds healed, he was transferred to Gonzales. That was a mistake. A lot of his shootings around Gonzales had been of blacks and damn Yankee soldiers, which was not an unpopular activity at the time. Friendly officials allowed Wes to escape.

Wes celebrated his freedom in a saloon that night by ventilating a gunman named Morgan (34). For this a sheriff named Jack Helms went after Hardin. Wes had never cottoned to Helms anyway. Wes thought he was in cahoots with the carpetbagging Reconstructionists, and he found it a distinct pleasure to have the opportunity to trade shots with Helms (35).

Though various chroniclers speak of Hardin's forty notches, none has ever specifically come up with more than thirty-six. This is not to say that Hardin did not earn forty. He did a mess of shooting and it could well be that a corpse here and there got lost in the shuffle. But no matter how the first thirty-nine notches are accounted for, there's no dispute about number 40, or, if we are going to be sticklers for detail, number 36. That was Deputy Sheriff Charley Webb of Brown County. Wes celebrated his twenty-first birthday on May 26, 1874, by going to the races at Comanche, where he won about $3,000.

Later, Hardin was in a saloon drinking when he was warned that Webb was after him. He just drank some more. Then Webb walked in, wearing two six-shooters in his waist. Wes reeled toward him. "Are you looking for me?" he asked.

Webb shook his head. "There ain't no reason why I should be," he said.

Hardin glared at him and said finally, "All right." He turned to order a drink when someone shouted, "Look out!"

Webb had drawn his guns and got off a quick shot at Hardin, catching him in the side. Wes came around in a spin and quickly drew and fired as he fell. The shot caught Webb squarely between the eyes.

There was now a $4,000 price on Hardin's head and he headed for points east. He moved through Louisiana to Alabama to Florida. He did a lot of gambling and drinking and some shooting, but was careful not to do any killing. Wes didn't want to do anything that would attract attention to the Hardin trademark. On August 23, 1877, Wes was on a train at Pensacola Junction, Florida, when two Texas Rangers overpowered and captured him as he went for his gun.

Wes Hardin was sentenced to twenty-five years in prison but did only fifteen years before he was released, in 1894. With Reconstruction over, Hardin was granted a full pardon.

On August 19, 1895, Wes was in the Acme Saloon on San Antonio Street in El Paso. He had made an enemy of old John Selman, the constable, a tough and mean gunfighter in his own right. It was obvious the dislike would eventually be settled with lead. Hardin was standing at the bar when Selman walked in. Hardin looked up and saw Selman in the mirror. It was the last thing he ever saw. Selman drew and shot Wes through the back of the head.

There was a hearing on the shooting but Selman got off by claiming self-defense. He said that when he realized Hardin had seen him in the mirror, he figured Wes would whirl around shooting. So Selman said he had simply shot first—in self-defense—before he became number 41 or 37 or whatever.

Five Really Perfect Crimes

1. In the Groove. The greatest bank robber this country ever produced was George Leonidas Leslie, who masterminded 80 percent of the bank burglaries committed in the United States from 1864 to 1884, when he was murdered. One of Leslie's most successful techniques involved the "Little Joker," a steel-wire contraption that could be fitted inside the combination knob of a bank safe. Leslie would enter a bank, force off the knob on the safe, insert the Little Joker, and then depart, leaving no indication of any intrusion. The safe would be used for a couple of weeks and the wires would cut grooves under the dial every time the combination was worked. Then Leslie would break in again, take off the knob, and study the grooves. He had the combination numbers and by trial and error could deduce the right sequence. The safe would then be opened and thoroughly cleaned out by Leslie's mob. Authorities would suspect an inside job and Leslie didn't give them any reason to think differently. Sometime later, he would slip into the bank a third time and remove his special wire gadget. It took safemakers years to figure out how their safes were constantly being opened.

2. Clues, Clues, Clues. One of the most perplexing murders still in the unsolved files is that of Leila Welsh, a twenty-year-old girl who lived in Kansas City, Missouri. At about three o'clock in the morning, on March 9, 1941, the killer entered her first-floor bedroom through a window. He crushed in both sides of her head with a blunt instrument, then slashed her throat and other parts of her body with a knife. The violence of the attack indicated to police that the killer was probably someone with an intense hatred for the girl. Yet investigation showed that the well-educated, serious-minded girl had no close men friends and no known enemies.

No motive for the crime was ever established and no tangible clues were found—and for a very good reason. To frustrate the law, the killer had planted dozens of phony clues at the scene and in the backyard. First, authorities found a man's shirt and a pair of trousers that were eventually traced to a very prominent man in Kansas City. They had been thrown into a garbage can and retrieved by the killer. A butcher knife that was not the murder weapon was found, but it bore fingerprints of another innocent man. Then a stonemason's hammer was discovered, which also had not been used in the assault. A pair of white gloves had the victim's blood on them, but it was clear that the killer had not worn them while committing the crime; he had smeared them afterward. He then littered the murder room with no fewer than fifty cigarette butts, some bearing lipstick, and dropped a book of matches with a phone number written inside. It, too, was traced to another innocent man. If the killer accidentally left any real clues behind, they were lost among all the phony ones—or perhaps were dismissed by the police as being false leads.

3. A Toast to Crime. The thirstiest criminal on record was a French thief who bewildered a Paris distillery for more than two decades. For years the firm was puzzled by a steady loss of liquor from its plants and could find no explanation for it, even after instituting a close watch of employees to make sure they were not smuggling out the spirits. An alert police inspector solved the mystery by ordering one of the distillery vats emptied. At the bottom he found an odd apparatus with a runoff pipe. The pipe ran into a small, shored-up tunnel, just large enough for a man's body, and then to a garage some 200 yards away, where the ingenious thief had merely poured himself a liter when he got the thirst. When arrested, the culprit was insulted at the charge that he had sold the spirits for profit, insisting he had consumed the estimated 5,000 gallons in stolen liquor all by himself.

4. Who Stole the Dingdong? At the Chicago World's Fair of 1893, the Daughters of the American Revolution exhibited a bell that was a reproduction of the Liberty Bell. The bogus bell, which contained the metal of a quarter of a million pennies contributed by schoolchildren from all over the country, was six feet tall and weighed six and a half tons. Plans had been made to take the bell on tour when the fair ended, but someone else had other ideas. One day, just before the fair was over, the bell disappeared from the exhibit and was never seen again. How it was moved secretly and got past the security guards is a mystery never solved.

5. Come and Get It. In 1880 the Bank of England took up new quarters in London and claimed it now had "the world's most impregnable bank vault." A few weeks later, a laborer, after a bit of fuss, was allowed into the office of the bank president. He made the seemingly ridiculous claim that a thief, knowing a certain secret, could enter and leave the bullion room as often as he wanted. The president laughed but finally agreed to the man's proposal to come to the bank that midnight and open the vault. The president and several associates did so and were flabbergasted to find the laborer sitting inside the vault on a pile of gold bars. The bank officials promptly paid the man $4,000 for the secret of how he'd done it. He explained that one day, while doing repair work on a nearby sewer, he had discovered and crawled into an unused drainpipe. Noticing a ladder, he climbed up it, pushed up a trapdoor, and found himself inside what had been heralded as an impregnable bank vault.

II.
THE
MONEY TAKERS

The Money Takers #1

One of the most imaginative swindles was created by a mail-order fraudster who advertised "a method 100% effective against cockroaches when used as directed." Those who sent in their money received a package containing two wooden blocks, marked A and B, and a set of instructions. The instructions read: "Put Block A on a flat surface. Place cockroach on Block A. Now take Block B and strike down on Block A with good force." When used as directed, this method did indeed prove 100 percent effective.

Nonetheless, U.S. postal authorities, notorious for lacking a sense of humor, sent the mail-order con artist to jail for fraud.

The Money Takers #2

"Dear Sir:
"As a service to regular churchgoers such as yourself, we have printed an easy-to-read Bible which will sell in bookstores at $19.95. However, we are sending a leatherette-bound edition for $5. If you prefer the deluxe leather edition at half the usual price, return the leatherette version with an extra $5."

This is the way the letter reads in the newest wrinkle in the unordered-merchandise racket. Shortly, the Bible with a bill for five dollars arrives, and very few people refuse to buy it. Instead of a leatherette-bound book, they get the deluxe version. Thinking the publisher has made a mistake, from which they can benefit, they rush off a check. The racket men have learned a long time ago there's a bit of larceny even in the most devout of us.

The Money Takers #3

Really good pickpockets have an uncanny and unerring "grift sense," which permits them to anticipate what the victim will do next. For example, the thief may rest his forearm against the back of his victim's shoulders in a crowd to keep him from getting too close. Then his free hand will lightly fan the back pocket or another pocket to locate the exact position of the wallet. Should the victim get suspicious, the muscles along the spine will tighten, and the pickpocket feels the reaction through his forearm. The crook also watches for a reddening of the skin below and behind the ears. By the time the victim goes for his pocket the pickpocket's hand is no longer there and the wallet is safe—for the moment. But the crook's hand comes right back, for even if the mark is still nervous or suspicious, he will be too embarrassed to grab for his wallet a second time, it would look too much as though he suspected the man behind him of being a thief.

The Money Takers #4

What's the easiest way to pass a bad check? Get drunk. One professional rubber-check artist, now doing time, used this routine steadily. He'd walk into a bar, drink enough drinks to make appearing cockeyed plausible, act careless with his change, and then ask the bartender to cash a check for him. Normally a bartender might ask for proof of the check's authenticity, but now he just saw dollar signs. He would cash the check eagerly—and shortchange the drunk five or ten dollars. Sometimes the so-called drunk put on such a good act that another patron would cash his check for him before the bartender could. He, too, could not resist the crook's invitation to larceny. Some check passers have admitted to police that they have made as much as $25,000 a year with just the drunk dodge.

The Money Takers #5

At a Las Vegas gathering of a number of the leading gamblers in the country a few years ago, a newspaper reporter asked them to name the most common gambling gyp of all. The winner was the spinning-coin game. It was estimated that this game, played dishonestly, had gypped Americans of an estimated $100 million over the years. A stranger will ask if you want to bet him which way a coin will land, heads or tails, if it is spun on, say, a bar, table, or army footlocker. Just to prove that everything is on the level, he hands you the quarter for you to spin. He calls it right every time. The secret is a nick on one edge. When the coin is spun, the hustler can tell the difference between the edges and thus make the right call. In a variation on this, the hustler has a coin that he can control when he spins it. When his opponent spins it, he merely has to watch how he is holding the coin. Half the circumference of the coin has been beveled to the head side and the other half to the tail side, so that the coin when spun with the beveled-head side down will always come up tails, and vice versa. The victim thinks he is handling a normally worn coin.

III.
PUNISHMENTS AND EXECUTIONS

Seven First-Night Reviews of the First Electrocution

William Kemmler was really quite a pedestrian murderer, having on the night of March 28, 1889, taken an ax and cracked the skull of his mistress, Tillie Ziegler. Ordinarily, the Buffalo, New York, murderer would have been speedily hanged, buried, and forgotten. Instead, becoming a pawn in a great billion-dollar battle between two great industrial giants, he won lasting fame as the first man to die in the electric chair.

Thomas A. Edison had developed the first electric power system in 1882 with the use of low-tension, direct current. Then, two years later, along came George Westinghouse with his alternating-current system, which was much easier and less costly to install than the heavy, expensive installation needed for DC. Realizing he was faced with a competing product far superior to his own for many purposes, Edison felt that his best hope was to disparage AC in the public's mind.

Edison decided to paint AC as a death-dealing system, and he sent out a young engineer, H. P. Brown, to put on shows around the country. Brown could set up an AC generator and electrocute stray dogs and cats and even horses. The flabbergasted audience were left in grim fear of AC. Then Brown took his death show to the New York legislature, hoping to get AC banned. Instead the legislature, having already banned hanging as too cruel and seeking a method to replace it, decided the perfect alternative had been found. George Westinghouse was appalled. He felt that if his system was used to execute people, it would never gain acceptance in the household. It was an open secret that Westinghouse spent $100,000 in the legal fight to save the man so condemned, Kemmler.

But all legal maneuvers failed and Kemmler's execution

date was set. By this time Kemmler was caught up in the spirit of things and thought of his role as that of a martyr to science.

On the morning of August 6, 1890, Kemmler was led into the execution chamber at Auburn State Prison and formally introduced by the warden to the 27 witnesses. One later wrote, "His manner indicated a state of subdued elation, as if he were gratified at being the central figure of the occasion."

When the guards trembled as they adjusted the straps, Kemmler said, "Now, take your time, boys, and do it right. We don't want to take any chances with this thing, you know."

When the head electrode was placed in position, Kemmler wiggled a bit and said, "I guess you'd better make that a little tighter."

The execution was hideously bungled. The current danced between 700 and 1,200 volts. After Kemmler was pronounced dead, all hell broke loose. The New York *World* reported: "Suddenly the breast heaved. There was a straining at the straps which bound him. . . . The man was alive! Warden, physicians, everybody, lost their wits. There was a startled cry for the current to be turned on again. Signals only half understood were given to those in the next room at the switchboard. When they knew what had happened, they were prompt to act and the switch-handle could be heard as it pulled back and forth, breaking the current into jets."

This time the current ran for seventy seconds, much too long, and the body was badly burned. During this second ordeal two of the witnesses, including George G. Bain of the United Press, fainted and another retched and bolted from the room.

This time Willie Kemmler was dead.

Naturally, the next-day "reviews" of the grisly show were not good:

> 1. Buffalo *Express:* "Kemmler will be the last man executed in such a manner."
> 2. New York *World:* "So long as it stands, conviction for capital offenses will be difficult to the point of impossibility. Juries will not willingly condemn men to death by torture."
> 3. New York *Times:* "A sacrifice to the whims and theories of the coterie of cranks and politicians who induced the legislature of the state to supplant

hanging by electrical execution was offered up today in the person of William Kemmler, the Buffalo murderer. He died this morning under the most revolting circumstances, and with his death there was placed to the discredit of the State of New York an execution that was a disgrace to civilization."

4. London *Times:* "It is impossible to imagine a more revolting exhibition."

5. London *Standard:* "A disgrace to humanity."

6. London *Chronicle:* "Worthy of the darkest chambers of the Inquisition in the 16th century."

7. George Westinghouse: "They could have done better with an ax."

However, as is often also the case with Broadway reviews, the critics proved wrong. The electric chair has had a very long run.

Fourteen Strange Punishments

1. Tragic Whistle. Undoubtedly the worst punishment for a meaningless crime was that meted out to Marie-Augustin, marquis de Pelier, of Brittany. As a youth of twenty-two he had made the mistake of whistling at Marie Antoinette as she was taking her seat in the royal box of the Comédie Française. For this offense he was branded "a prisoner of state" and sentenced to solitary confinement in a local prison. Four years later, in 1790, Pelier was secretly transferred to the Lourdes dungeon. The chaos of the French Revolution and the executions of Louis XVI and Marie Antoinette did not end Pelier's incarceration. In fact, he continued to languish in solitary confinement for another twenty-four years. Then, after the overthrow of Napoleon, a new royal procurator, going over the prison records, discovered Pelier was still there. Papers were drawn up for his release, but just then Napoleon chose to escape to Elba, and France was again in turmoil. Pelier's case was forgotten. It was not until 1836 that Pelier was finally released. By that time he had served fifty years, most of it in solitary confinement, for a wolf whistle.

2. Death to the Statues. In Foochow, China, in 1900, a man was killed when one of fifteen wooden Buddhist statues fell from a temple ledge and killed him. Since the dead man's family had much influence, they were able to have the offending statue, as well as the other fourteen, tried for murder. The statues were promptly found guilty and all were beheaded in a somber public execution.

3. The Branded Hand. Until 1844 branding of criminals was practiced in this country. The last man thus punished was Jonathan Walker, who had the initials SS, for Slave Stealer, burned into the palm of his right hand. Walker had tried to help seven slaves escape to the Bahamas. Whittier wrote his poem *The Man with the Branded Hand* about this case.

4. Stand-in. Those people who argue against capital punishment might well cite the penalty handed out for murder among the Agbede tribesmen of Africa. The killer of another man must transform himself into the image of his victim. He takes over the victim's station in life, his property, his duties and functions. If the victim was married, the murderer must marry the widow.

5. Hanging Around. James Mossman was hanged in Galloway, Scotland, in 1785 for two bizarre reasons: He was a resident of the next district, and he was found on the highway without good reason.

6. Fitting the Crime. Among the Roman emperors, Gallienus (A.D. 253–268) was probably the most ingenious at making the punishment fit the crime. Angered by a jewel dealer who had sold his wife gems that were imitations, he ordered the dishonest man to be thrown to the lions in the arena. The event played before a packed house and the jeweler, half dead with fright, literally had to be carried in. While the man trembled the door to a large, closed cage was slowly opened. The hushed crowd waited. Instead of a lion, out stepped a small chicken. Then Gallienus' proclamation was read: "He practiced deceit and has had it practiced on him." The jeweler had to be carried from the arena.

7. Labeled. In the back country of Cambodia unfaithful wives are punished by having the figure of a man tattooed on their cheeks. Both the French, earlier, and now the Communists have been unable to halt the practice.

8. The Unforgiving. In 1821, at the age of twenty-four, Anthony Panizzi, later to become librarian of the British Museum, escaped from his native Italy, where he was about to be executed as a revolutionary. He thought he'd put the whole ugly business behind him. Soon, however, he received a dunning letter from his government, which demanded reimbursement for the cost of erecting the gallows and the payment promised to the hangman.

9. The Squaw Man's Fate. On September 30, 1878, Indians of the White River Ute tribe of Colorado staged the famous Meeker Massacre, killing Indian agent Nathan C. Meeker and all other male members of his agency. One Indian, Yogia, refused to take part in the raid, and the tribe found him guilty of desertion. His penalty, extremely harsh for an Indian, was to lead the life of a woman. He was sentenced to wear squaw clothing and perform squaw work for the rest of his life, humiliating conditions that lasted for sixty years, until 1938.

10. Death of a Witch. Of all the inhumane methods of execution used in this country, eighty-year-old Giles Corey suffered the worst. Refusing even to answer the charges of witchcraft brought against him in Salem, Massachusetts, in 1692, he automatically brought on himself the penalty for remaining mute—being pressed to death. Secured to the ground, Corey refused to say anything other than "More weight" as the executioner continued to pile heavy rocks on his chest. The brutality of Corey's execution and his heroic actions are credited as having helped to build the public revulsion that finally ended the witchcraft trials.

11. Schoolmaster in Chains. Because he suffered from frequent fits of insanity, schoolmaster Samuel Coolidge often was locked up in chains. The selectmen of Watertown, Massachusetts, however, beginning in 1751, continued to reappoint him each year to his post. He was permitted to teach school during his periods of sanity.

12. You Can't Go Home Again. One of the most pathetic prisoners in American history was Martin Dalton, who was sentenced to life for murder. After spending thirty-two years in the Rhode Island State Prison, he was offered a pardon in 1930. Dalton refused it, explaining he had no family to return to and no place else to go. He remained in prison another thirty years and died in 1960. During the last sixty-one years of his sixty-two years in prison, Dalton did not have a single visitor and for the last twenty-one years did not receive even a letter.

13. Sentenced to Be Unread. On July 14, 1789, the Bastille in Paris was stormed by the mobs during the French Revolution, and hundreds and hundreds of prisoners were released. Few, however, proved to be human. The vast number of prisoners turned out to be . . . books. The books had contained criticisms of the four previous kings of France and these monarchs, outraged, had ordered the books confiscated and locked up in the Bastille forever.

14. Act of Rebellion. Probably the strangest reason for executing a soldier was the charge brought against Private John Wilson of the 84th Yorkshire and Lancaster Regiment of the British Army. His sole offense was refusing to accept his daily ration of rum, which was labeled an "act of rebellion." At his court-martial in Bangalore, India, in November 1815, it was brought out that Wilson was a lifelong nondrinker. Despite this, he was found guilty and shot.

Nine Hanging Dramas

1. Die Now, Argue Later. In the frontier West, law and order came slowly, but justice, after a fashion, came fast. If a man committed murder or any other of the numerous crimes considered capital offenses, he seldom lived to see another sunset. The first murder trial in the Republic of Texas was held in 1836, and the defendant was found guilty and sentenced to be hanged. The defense attorney immediately gave notice of his intention to appeal, and was told dryly by the judge: "Go right ahead and appeal, but in the meantime the prisoner is going to be hanged." And he was.

2. The Big Sleep. At Sutter Creek, California, during the gold-rush days, a card dealer carved up a miner who had objected to the way the aces were falling. He was tried and convicted within the hour and given seventy-five lashes with a cat-o'-nine-tails. The next day, the wounded miner died and the dealer was subjected to another quick trial, even though he lay slumped over a table and heard none of the proceedings. Found guilty, he was taken out and hanged while he was still unconscious from the lashing.

3. Act of Mercy. Sometimes hangings in the Old West were carried out even faster than intended. Judge Robert M. "Three-Legged Willie" Williamson of Texas was said to possess a tender heart under his stern exterior. Once he asked a prisoner if he had "any reason why the sentence of death should not be pronounced upon you." The prisoner turned sickly pale and was struck speechless with fear. According to a contemporary account, his "eyeballs literally started from their sockets in view of the appalling sentence." Judge Williamson studied the man and then, the local newspaper reported, "melted in sympathy." He signaled to the sheriff and said, "I think you had better take him out and hang him now. He has lost all consciousness and sensibility and his neck can be broken without his knowing or feeling it."

4. A Good Execution. A code of chivalry in the West allowed men to die bravely if they wanted to. When Andrew J. Huff was hanged in Surprise Valley, Nevada, he was first allowed to shake hands with his friends in the crowd and then, with his hands still free, allowed to climb upon a fence underneath the temporary gallows. Huff placed the noose around his own neck and tightened it just the way he wanted. The crowd waited patiently while Huff enjoyed some last personal thoughts and then jumped from the fence, playing the part of his own hangman.

5. The Long Hanging. Some Western hangings were conducted inhumanely, especially when the crime was one the community really wanted to discourage. Horse stealing was considered such an offense in Dodge City in the 1870s. When a horse thief was convicted he was trussed up, put on the horse he'd stolen, and taken out of town to a place called the "cottonwoods." The hanging tree was a large, dead cottonwood from which hung more than a dozen nooses. Some still held skeletons and the bones of other victims lay on the ground under the empty nooses. A noose was fashioned by one member of the hanging party and tossed over a high limb; then the rope was slipped over the thief's head and tightened. The rope was then anchored to another limb. Often the condemned man's lips would move in prayer as he waited for the horse to be whipped out from under him. But it didn't happen. The condemned man would stare in amazement as he saw his executioners ride off. Had they just been toying with him? But soon the weight of his awful punishment would sink in. He was to face death as long as he could. He could watch the buzzards as they circled, waiting to begin their feast.

The man would live just as long as the horse remained under him. Of course, if he wished, he could spur the animal out from under him and end his misery. But he wouldn't do that. There was a chance that someone would happen by, take pity on him, and turn him loose. Hope would keep the man alive but torture him every second. The sun would set and night would fall, but the man wouldn't be able to sleep. What if the horse took a notion to walk away? He could hear wolves in the distance. If one of them neared, the horse would shy and that would be the end. With the first rays of morning the man would be physically and mentally exhausted. The sun would burn him. He prayed he could hold out until night again. He prayed the horse would also. The animal, too, would be growing thirsty and hungry and weary of the deadweight on its back. Almost never did the horse hold still through another day. As he would slip out from under the man on its back, there would be a weak cry. The man's heels, only a foot or so from the ground, would kick as, in agony, he strangled slowly to death. Horse thieving remained one of the West's most prevalent crimes, but it soon became extinct around Dodge City.

6. The Unrepentant. Few condemned persons have gone to their death as defiantly as Frankie Silvers, the first white woman ever legally hanged in North Carolina. In 1831 she hacked her husband to death with an ax while he was sleeping, cut up and burned the body, and later showed little remorse. When she mounted the gallows, she munched on a piece of cake and wouldn't let the execution proceed until she had eaten every last crumb.

7. Choice. In thirteenth-century France a man to be hanged as a habitual thief could win his release if a maiden would step forth and offer to marry him. When Jean Poqueron of Hautvilliers was about to be hanged in Reims in 1234, an orphan girl, quite homely, stepped forward. Poqueron took one look at her and shook his head. "No," he said. "I'd rather marry the gallows. Hangman, do your duty." He was duly executed.

8. The Man They Couldn't Hang. John Lee was led to the scaffold in Exeter, England, on a cold, windy morning in February 1895, before about 100 witnesses. The signal was given and the hangman released the mechanism that held the trapdoor shut but . . . nothing happened. Lee stood there, a mask over his bowed head, waiting to be dropped to eternity. The hangman pulled the trigger again. Still nothing. The hangman hurried under the scaffold to look for the trouble. Someone finally thought to lead Lee back off the trapdoor to await developments. The hangman reset the door and tried the mechanism. It worked perfectly. Lee was returned to his position on the trapdoor. The drop was again triggered . . . and nothing happened.

The crowd, angry at the official incompetence, began to mumble. Lee was led back to his cell, still with the hood over his head. Meanwhile the warden stood on the trapdoor, holding on to the hands of guards on the either side of the door. The trapdoor worked perfectly, leaving the warden dangling in the air. With things now working fine again, Lee was brought back to the scaffold. For a third time the trapdoor was triggered . . . and once again Lee remained standing there. A fourth time . . . and still nothing happened.

By now the crowd was turning ugly, and the hangman, warden, and guards were very nervous. The attempted execution seemed to be defying some hidden force. The trapdoor worked fine only when John Lee was not standing on it. Finally, the sheriff stepped forward and ordered the execution stopped so that he could make a report to higher authorities. A report reached the Home Secretary, and the issue was eventually debated in Parliament. Since it was agreed that John Lee had gone through terrible anguish during his bungled "execution," his death sentence was commuted to life imprisonment. A few years later, the sentence was further reduced and Lee walked out a free man. For years he toured Europe and the United States, appearing onstage as the Man They Couldn't Hang.

No acceptable explanation for the trapdoor's malfunction was ever found, despite a lengthy scientific investigation. The explanation the public preferred was Lee's own: "I have always had a feeling that I had help from some Power greater than gravity."

9. Neutral Zone. A case of criminals falling out is probably best illustrated by a pair of English murderers, Albert Milsom and Henry Fowler. Milsom, arrested for the robbery-murder of an old man, collapsed when he saw the police. He quickly confessed and implicated Fowler as his accomplice, a fact that the latter did not appreciate. When brought in to confront Milsom, the enraged Fowler almost broke free, even though he was handcuffed and being restrained by several officers. In court, after the pair heard the death sentence, Fowler sprang across the dock, trying to get his manacled hands around his companion's throat.

The pair were to be hanged with another murderer, a man named Seaman. It was decided that Seaman would be placed between the feuding killers on the gallows platform. When Seaman saw the arrangement, he laughed loudly. "I've been many things in my life," he said, "but this is the first time I've been a peacemaker."

Ten Pros and Cons on Capital Punishment

1. Life shall go for life, eye for eye, tooth for tooth, hand for hand, foot for foot.—*Deuteronomy, XIX:21*

2. I shall ask for the abolition of the punishment of death until I have the infallibility of human judgment demonstrated to me.—*Thomas Jefferson*

3. The worst form of assassination, because . . . it is invested with the approval of society.—*George Bernard Shaw*

4. The infliction of public vengeance.—*John Calvin*

5. Only an administrative murder.—*Albert Camus*

6. If the desire to kill and the opportunity to kill always came together, who would escape hanging?—*Mark Twain*

7. No one knows how many innocent men, erroneously convicted of murder, have been put to death by American governments. For, once a convicted man is dead, all interest in vindicating him generally evaporates.—*Judge Jerome Frank*

8. It is well for our vanity that we slay the criminal, for if we suffered him to live he might show us what we had gained by his crime.—*Oscar Wilde*

9. The manner in which society rids itself of cancer cells.—*Anonymous*

10. People who deserve it always believe in capital punishment.—*Lincoln Steffens*

Five Mass Murderers and Where They Are Now

If Juan Corona never goes back to prison, his fate will not be at all unusual for a mass murderer. Only about half such men are sent to prison; many others have been judged not sane in the legal sense—thus not fit to stand trial—and have been sent to mental institutions. Here is the fate of some recent mass killers.

1. Son of Sam. In 1978 David Berkowitz, New York City's Son of Sam, pleaded guilty to all the murders he was charged with. The judge ruled that Berkowitz was not competent to stand trial and had him confined to a state psychiatric center.

2. Howard Unruh. In 1949 Unruh stepped out of his home in a quiet, working-class neighborhood in East Camden, New Jersey, and purportedly shot to death the shoemaker, the druggist, the barber, a six-year-old in the barber chair, a two-year-old watching from a window, and eight other neighbors. Later, he said, "They were making derogatory remarks about my character." Unable to stand trial, Unruh was committed to Trenton State Hospital as a psychotic with a persecution complex. Today, at fifty-seven, he is reported to be a withdrawn, quiet man who "mostly reads or sits around."

3. Lorne Acquin. In July 1977 the bodies of Cheryl Beaudoin, aged twenty-nine, and eight children, aged four to twelve, were found in the Beaudoins' home in Prospect, Connecticut. Lorne Acquin, twenty-seven, a foster brother of the dead woman's husband, was charged with the murders. Acquin was committed to the state mental hospital in Middletown, having been diagnosed as suffering from "schizophrenia or a type of epilepsy that makes him dangerous to himself or others."

4. Ronald De Feo, Jr. In November 1974 Ronald De Feo, Jr., twenty-three, shot to death his mother, father, two sisters, and two brothers while they slept. The best-seller *The Amityville Horror* relates the experiences of the next owners of the De Feo house, allegedly haunted by ghosts. De Feo claimed insanity as a defense but was sentenced in 1975 to 150 years in prison. Officials at the state prison at Dannemora say he is in the "general population" and doing maintenance work.

5. Elmer Wayne Henley. In 1974 Elmer Wayne Henley was convicted in Texas of the homosexual torture-murders of twenty-seven youths. He was sentenced to 594 years in the prison at Huntsville.

Six Tombstones That Bespeak Violence

1. In a Cripple Creek, Colorado, cemetery:
   He Called Bill Smith a Liar

2. In Oak Hill Cemetery, Tama, Iowa:
   TAYLOR—Assassinated July 19, 1913, by a Dirty Coward
   Whose Name Is Not Worthy to Be Mentioned Here

3. In Boot Hill Cemetery, Tombstone, Arizona:
   HERE LIES LESTER MOORE
   FOUR SLUGS FROM A FORTY-FOUR
   NO LES
   NO MOORE

4. On the tombstone of a smuggler who was hanged in Larne, Ireland:
   RAB McBETH
   WHO DIED FOR THE WANT OF ANOTHER BREATH
   1791–1823

5. On a tombstone in Ruidoso, New Mexico:
> HERE LIES WILD BILL BRITT
> RAN FOR SHERIFF IN '82
> RAN FROM SHERIFF IN '83
> BURIED IN '84

6. In a cemetery in Dillstein, Germany, there is a gravestone in the form of a cross on which is engraved an ax. Buried there is an ax a young man had used to kill his twin brother.

Four Thoughts on Hanging

1. No man is so good as not to deserve hanging ten times over were he to submit all his thoughts and actions to the laws.—*Montaigne.*

2. To choke a poor scamp for the glory of God.—*James Russell Lowell*

3. Beware when your lawyer promises he will get you a suspended sentence; you may be hanged.—*Anonymous*

4. Executions are intended to draw spectators. If they do not draw spectators they don't answer their purpose.—*Samuel Johnson.*

Six "Wrong Men"

1. Clerical Boner. On a wintry day in 1902 a noose was put around the neck of J. B. Brown; he was to be hanged for the murder of Harry Wesson. He kept protesting his innocence, but it was too late. His case had gone all the way to the Florida Supreme Court and all had been denied. In accordance with state law, the sheriff began to read the death warrant. The words of doom descended on Brown's ears. He weakly shook his head as a last protest that he was not guilty. Suddenly the sheriff stopped reading. He motioned to other officials to look at the paper. Brown stood there helplessly. He thought he heard one official say, "Let's hang him anyway." But the sheriff was opposed, saying the law was the law. Suddenly they took the rope from Brown's neck and his hands were cut free. They led him back to his cell. Only then was he told what had happened.

Through a clerical error, Brown's name was not on the death warrant. Instead there was the name of the foreman of the jury that had convicted him. The story created a nationwide stir. People said that what Brown had gone through was worse than being hanged. Pressure mounted on the governor to commute his sentence to life and he did so. For the next eleven years Brown claimed to be innocent. Then, in 1913, a man named J. J. Johnson made a deathbed confession that he had killed Wesson. The confession checked out fully as Johnson even revealed where he'd hidden some of the murder victim's effects. Brown won a pardon and financial compensation of $2,492—to be doled out in $25 monthly installments.

2. Slipped Knot. Will Purvis' escape from execution for a crime he hadn't committed was startling. Purvis was slated to be hanged in Mississippi on February 7, 1894, and hundreds gathered for the spectacle. Many in the crowd were sure Purvis was innocent but now it was too late to do anything. They could only show support for Purvis by being there at the end. As the trap was sprung the knot around Purvis' neck slipped and he dropped unharmed. The execution was postponed because the crowd got unruly. Many took the event as a sign from God that Purvis was innocent. During this postponement friends of Purvis helped him to escape from jail. He later surrendered to a new governor, who commuted his sentence to life. It took twenty-two more years, until 1920, to prove Purvis was innocent, once again thanks to a deathbed confession. For all his woes, Purvis was awarded $5,000.

3. The Thirty-Year Torment. Near Minot, North Dakota, the body of a man was found hanging from a tree. He was a farmhand named Charles Herzog. There was a note pinned to his coat that read, "When my body is found, please notify my mother, Mrs. Kathryn Herzog. A letter in my pocket will reveal the secret of my wretched life. I can bear it no longer."

Officials broke the seal to that letter, and those who had been around three decades earlier remembered another hanging—this one a legal execution. The hanged man was Charles Sterling, convicted of the rape-murder of a young girl named Lizzie Grombacker. In his letter Herzog confessed to the crime. He even indicated where the veil worn by the girl on the day of the slaying could be found. Police checked and were able to identify the veil as hers. Charles Sterling was a "wrong man" who didn't survive.

4. The Live Corpse. In August 1925, twenty-year-old Mary Vickery disappeared from the small mining town of Coxton, Kentucky. A few months later, a body was found and then identified as Mary's. A thirty-one-year-old cabdriver, Condy Dabney, was arrested. The chief witness against him was a woman named Marie Jackson. She testified that she and Mary Vickery had gone for a ride out of town with Dabney and that the three had then sat on a hill in a place called Ivy Hill. After a while, she said, Mary and the man had gone off because they wanted to be alone. She said she was still able to see them, however, and saw Mary resist his advances. Then, went the story, Dabney hit the girl over the head with a stick and, as she lay motionless, criminally assaulted her. He then dragged the girl into the entrance of a mine shaft, where a body was later found. Marie Jackson said she cowered in the underbrush through all this and when Dabney found her, he warned her never to say what had happened or he would kill her, too. For his part, Dabney denied even knowing the Vickery girl. He did know Marie Jackson.

Dabney was found guilty and sentenced to life imprisonment. Actually, the story that Marie Jackson told was all a lie. Dabney could have been cleared by another woman, but she had not appeared at his trial—Mary Vickery, who wasn't dead. That was determined a year later when her name was spotted on a hotel register in another Kentucky town by a sharp-eyed patrolman. She was located and, yes, she was the right Mary Vickery; she said she didn't even know Marie Jackson. That woman later admitted she hated Dabney and drew a prison term for false swearing. But why hadn't Mary Vickery come forward when she heard that a man had been charged with her murder? She said she just couldn't be bothered.

5. The Jackpot. On the surface, at least, Bertram Campbell was compensated for his "wrong man" nightmare. Despite his impeccable past, he had been convicted of forgery on the testimony of five bank tellers. He served almost four years of a five-to-ten-year sentence in Sing Sing before the real culprit, master forger Alexander Thiel, was caught. On June 17, 1946, Campbell was awarded $75,000 for his "humiliation" and $40,000 for "lost wages." It seemed that Campbell's misfortune had turned to luck. Just eighty-two days later, however, the years of anxiety and imprisonment took their toll on a sick and broken Bertram Campbell, and he died. But even more misfortune had preceded his death. It was learned that when the $115,000 had been turned over to Campbell for the terrible injustice done him, other officials had slapped him with a bill for several thousand dollars for welfare money given to his wife during the time he had been falsely imprisoned!

6. "That's My Man." Perhaps the strangest case of mistaken identity happened in Haverstraw, New York, a number of years ago. A man named Hoag came to town and acquired a job, a large circle of friends, and a wife. Six months later, he got out of town just ahead of the police. It had been discovered that he already had a wife in another city. Then, two years later, a man named Parker settled in Haverstraw, and suddenly was arrested on a charge of bigamy. More than a dozen witnesses identified Parker as Hoag. Hoag's former employer would know him anywhere. And then there was Mrs. Hoag. She certainly could recognize her husband when she saw him. To clinch matters, Mrs. Hoag informed the court that her husband had a long red scar on his right foot. Parker promptly took off both shoes and socks. There was no scar on either foot. The case was dismissed.

IV.
WORDS
OF WISDOM

Ten Quotable Quotes

1. Leave him be, Kid. A man with his nerve deserves not to be shot.—*Butch Cassidy to the Sundance Kid about a guard who refused to open a train safe*

2. Why, honey, I wasn't going to kill that nice old man. He was white-headed.—*Bonnie Parker explaining to Clyde Barrow why she refused his order to shoot a man trying to throw a log in front of their getaway car*

3. We only kill each other.—*Bugsy Siegel*

4. I'm sorry, but I'd rather blow the goddamn case.—*Frank Costello when asked by his lawyer to stop wearing $350 suits, which were hurting his case with the jury, and to switch to one from the rack*

5. It's too bad. I wanted to lend a hand with it.—*Murder Inc. hit man Pittsburgh Phil bemoaning the fact that he hadn't been around for a certain killing*

6. We were victims of circumstances. We were drove to it, sir.—*Cole Younger of the James Younger gang*

7. I don't believe in divorce.—*Carl Wanderer, a Chicago murderer, telling a reporter why he killed his wife instead of getting a separation*

8. We're bigger than U.S. Steel.—*Meyer Lansky on the syndicate*

9. Ballplayers don't kill people. In all my experience I cannot think of a single baseball player who ever killed anybody—at least so viciously as in this case.—*Attorney Alfred I. Rosner defending his client, Dasher Abbandando, a Murder Inc. killer and a second-baseman of some renown*

10. I wouldn't do that to a yellow dog.—*Al Capone when he got a peace offer from rival mobsters provided he let his*

henchmen, John Scalisi and Albert Anselmi, be "put on the spot" for the murder of Dion O'Banion. (That statement, reported in the press, brought this response from Chicago police captain John Stege: "There is no one on earth Capone wouldn't send to death if he thought his interests would be served"; a short time later, Scalisi and Anselmi were slain and peace reigned among the Chicago mobs.)

Three Famous Denials

1 Why, I'm a respectable businessman. I'm a secondhand dealer, I'm no gangster.—*Al Capone*

2. I'm no hood! And I don't like to be called a hood. I'm a thief.—*Alvin "Creepy" Karpis*

3. I am not a crook.—*Richard Nixon*

Fifteen Songs, Odes, Sayings, and Limericks on Crime

1. Lizzie Borden took an ax
   And gave her mother forty whacks;
   When she saw what she had done,
   She gave her father forty-one.
   —*Anonymous: (Lizzie Borden was accused but acquitted of murdering her stepmother and father in Fall River, Massachusetts, in 1892)*

2. There's no evidence of guilt,
   Lizzie Borden,

That should make your spirit wilt,
      Lizzie Borden;
   Many do not think that you,
   Chopped your father's head in two,
   It's so hard a thing to do,
      Lizzie Borden.
         —*A. L. Bixby*

3. It's not the people in prison who worry me. It's the people who aren't.—*Arthur Gore*

4. The reason the way of the transgressor is hard is because it's so crowded.—*Frank McKinney Hubbard*

5. Typewriter Heiress XXX's Out Husband.—*Headline in the Los Angeles* Times

6. Jesse James had a wife,
   She's a mourner all her life;
      His children they were brave;
   Oh, the dirty little coward
   That shot Mr. Howard
      Has laid poor Jesse in his grave.
         —*Anonymous song commemorating the death of Jesse James, who was living in St. Joseph, Missouri, under the name of Thomas Howard; Bob Ford shot him on April 3, 1882*

7. Laws are like cobwebs that entangle the weak, but are broken by the strong.—*Solon*

8. Prisons are built with stones of law, brothels with bricks of religion.—*William Blake*

9. Some day they'll go down together;
   They'll bury them side by side;
      To few it'll be grief—
      To the law a relief—
   But it's death for Bonnie and Clyde.
      —*Bonnie Parker*

10. The first prison I ever saw had inscribed on it "Cease to do evil; learn to do well"; but the inscription was on the outside, the prisoners could not read it.—*George Bernard Shaw*

11. Two brothers in our town did dwell:
    Hiram sought Heaven, but Isaac Sawtell.
    —*Anonymous, from* The Sawtell Murder, *on the 1890 murder in New Hampshire of Hiram Sawtell by his brother Isaac*

12. The criminal classes are so close to us that even the policeman can see them. They are so far away from us that only the poet can understand them.—*Oscar Wilde*

13. One murder makes a villain, millions a hero.—*Bishop Beilby Porteus*

14. When we want to read of the deeds done for love, whither do we turn? To the murder column; and there we are rarely disappointed.—*George Bernard Shaw*

15. The eagerness of a knave maketh him often as catchable as ignorance maketh a fool.—*Lord Halifax*

Eight More Quotable Quotes

1. Because that's where the money is.—*Willie Sutton when asked why he robbed banks*

2. From now on, you can call the five of us the Barbershop Quintet.—*Crazy Joe Gallo to a friend approaching a table where Gallo was sitting with four other men shortly after the barbershop murder of Albert Anastasia*

3. I am not a murderer, though I may be a bit peculiar.—*George Joseph Smith, the "Brides in the Bath" killer*

4. And another thing, Mama. When they kill us, don't ever say anything ugly about Clyde. Please promise me that. —*Bonnie Parker to her mother*

5. Poor Dorothy. Poor Dolores. Poor Grace. They all found out at one time or another that I was a crook and chose to

stick by me. I loved each one of them.—*Alvin Creepy Karpis on his molls*

6. My gun? Why, it's at home and ain't that a hell of a place for it.—*Doc Barker when arrested in Chicago*

7. The question of getting the right amount of sulphuric acid was only learned by experience.—*Murderer George Haigh on how to use acid to dispose of a body.*

8. Maybe I am getting lockjaw from being bit.—*Murder Inc. killer Pittsburgh Phil Strauss complaining that one of his victims bit him while struggling for his life*

Twenty-nine Last Words

1. Francis "Two-Gun" Crowley in the chair as the hood was placed over his head: "Give my love to mother."

2. Martin, a French innkeeper who did in many of his guests to steal their valuables, as he counted the house one night and said: "What a crowd. This will hurt business at the fair."

3. Mary Blandy, an eighteenth-century lass who fed her father arsenic: "Gentlemen, do not hang me high, for the sake of decency."

4. Sam Wilkinson, a New England slayer, noting several witnesses in attendance at his execution: "Who are these? Oh, gentlemen of the press. I hope we meet again. I'll keep a warm corner for you."

5. Deval, a French murderer, eagerly putting his head in position on the guillotine: "Hurry up, friend. Take my head. You can have it."

6. John Thurtell, an English felon, to the hangman: "Be sure to give me enough fall."

7. Delanoc, a Frenchman who killed his father and daughter, just as the guillotine blade was about to descend: "Good morning, world."

8. Sing Sing prisoner 68711, drumming his fingers impatiently on the arms of the electric chair while waiting for the end: "Step on the gas."

9. Sidney Etheridge, who axed an old woman to death and claimed her black cat had made him do it: "I've always had bad luck and black cats caused it. I'd like to have one of the black devils so I could hold him when they turn the juice on me." (Request denied.)

10. Harry Roberts, a New York slayer, to the prison doctor as he was strapped into the electric chair: "Doc, my last act is going to be for science. We'll see how fast this juice really works. The moment I feel it, I'll wiggle this finger." (It never wiggled.)

11. Lefroy, an Englishman who had a play produced the night before he was hanged: "Is there anything in the papers about my play?"

12. Anna Hahn, the Ohio multiple murderess who nursed her victims to death, disengaging her hand from the comforting one of the prison chaplain as she was strapped to the chair: "You might be killed, too, Father."

13. Bluebeard, Henri Landru: "Ah, well, it is not the first time that an innocent man has been condemned."

14. Bonjean, a French killer, to the audience at his execution: "A fine lot of suckers you are."

15. Joe Zangara, who killed Mayor Anton Cermak of Chicago while attempting to assassinate Franklin D. Roosevelt: "Go on, push the button. Push the button."

16. James Read, an English dandy who had killed a girl who wouldn't take a brush-off, insisting on going out properly when he noticed his clothing was awry: "Someone button my coat."

17. William Harper, a New York murderer, to the officer adjusting the straps to the electric chair: "What's the trouble, Sarge? Nervous?"

18. Sam Fooy, who bashed in the head of an Arkansas schoolteacher for the five dollars on his person, to the witnesses: "I'm as anxious to get out of this world as you people are to see me out of it."

19. Cipiore, a Frenchman told by his executioner to be calm: "I'd like to see you be calm if you were me."

20. Palmer, a notorious British prisoner, drawing back in mock horror from the trapdoor of the gallows: "Good heavens, do you think it's safe?"

21. John Dee Smith, killer of a Fort Worth, Indiana, restaurant owner during a holdup, to the warden just before the current was turned on: "I'll ask St. Peter if I can't come down and knock on your desk tomorrow to let you know everything is okay." (He didn't.)

22. Danton, one of the three great leaders of the French Revolution: "Afterward, show my head to the people. It is a head worth looking at."

23. Kidnapper and killer Bonnie Heady, in the gas chamber with her partner, Carl Austin Hall, asked the guards not to strap her man in too tightly: "You got plenty of room, honey?" Hall answered, "Yes, Mama." Then she smiled and awaited the deadly fumes.

24. Harry Farris, a Virginia killer, on two women accomplices who had squealed on him and thus escaped death with long prison sentences: "I only wish I never met those two tramps."

25. Barthelmy, a Frenchman executed in London: "Now I shall know the great secret."

26. Pat Carrigan, a Georgia bandit who killed his sweetheart because he feared he had told her too many incriminating details about his crimes, in the electric chair just before the current was turned on: "Don't! I am not as brave as I have pretended to be."

27. Chester S. Jordan, a Boston killer who had dissected his victim, to the warden in the death chamber: "I'm ready to die. All I ask is that you don't cut me up." (The required autopsy was performed.)

28. Poulman, a French slayer: "Put a franc in my pocket so the gravediggers can have a drink. It's a bitter, cold day."

29. Cherokee Bill, a Western badman: "I came to die, not to make a speech."

V.
INTERESTING METHODS OF SOLVING CRIMES

Six Men Who Had Psychic Experiences and Dreams That Solved Crimes

1. Don Sabel. Patrolmen Don Sabel and Robert Sass were on patrol on a late-fall afternoon in 1960 when the police dispatcher at Grosse Pointe Woods, Michigan, flashed a message about a couple who had been held up and robbed of cash and jewelry in their home. Descriptions of the two thieves were sketchy. For reasons he could not explain later, Officer Sabel told Sass to drive along Mack Street. Suddenly he stiffened and told Sass to pull over to the curb and stop. Sabel jumped out of the car and walked up to a man just about to enter a restaurant. He asked him a few questions and then frisked him. Finding a woman's wristwatch and $400 on the man, Sabel placed him under arrest. He took the suspect directly to the victims' home and they immediately identified him as one of the bandits and reclaimed the loot.

This was neither the first nor the last time that Don Sabel solved crimes in such a startling manner. Once, he noticed two men sitting in a car and for no definite reason decided to take them to headquarters for questioning. Meanwhile, a Mr. and Mrs. John Heberling called to report that their home had been burglarized. They didn't have to worry. Officer Sabel had already caught the guilty parties—and the loot—before the crime had even been reported. Many observers have labeled Sabel's achievements as supernatural premonitions. His chief once called them "pure inspiration." Sabel himself admitted that he couldn't explain them but preferred to call them hunches. One reporter noted, "He doesn't want to talk about it, but the steadily growing record speaks for itself."

2. Peter Hurkos. The casebook of Peter Hurkos, a Dutchman, bulges with remarkable psychic solutions. Once, Dutch police took him to a house where a man had been shot on his own doorstep. Hurkos fingered the victim's coat for a few moments and then told police that the killer was an older man, wore spectacles, had a mustache and a wooden leg, and had thrown the murder gun on the roof of the house. Police searched the roof and found the gun. They also found fingerprints on the gun that convicted the dead man's father-in-law—an older man who had a mustache, wore spectacles, and had a wooden leg.

On another occasion a firebug was terrorizing Nijmegen, Holland, and police, skeptical at first, asked Hurkos to help. He toured the scenes of several of the fires, finally finding a charred screwdriver handle. Then he said, "We must look for a boy—a boy in his teens." Still doubtful, the police supplied him with school-yearbook pictures of every boy in the city. Finally, Hurkos picked out one boy in a group shot. He was the son of a very prominent and wealthy man, and the police did not want to act. Hurkos insisted, telling them they would find a box of matches and a bottle of lighter fluid in the boy's pockets, even though he did not smoke. When the boy was brought in, he denied everything until Hurkos said, "Pull up the left leg of your overalls and show the police the scratches you got from the barbed-wire fence as you ran from the fire." The scratches were on his leg, and the boy broke down and confessed.

When the famed Stone of Scone was stolen from Westminster Abbey in 1950, Scotland Yard got nowhere until it invited the young but already famous Peter Hurkos to come to London. At the abbey, Hurkos fingered a tool left by the thieves; after several hours he said he could "see" the escape route the thieves had taken and drew a detailed map—even though he had never been in London before. He said the culprits were three men and a woman, and gave detailed descriptions of them, too. When all were arrested some months later, all four were found to match Hurkos' description.

In 1951 a wealthy man in Roubaix, France, could not find a tin box containing $30,000 in gold he had buried years before, when hoarding of gold was illegal. Now the law had been repealed. Stunned when he couldn't find the gold, he offered Hurkos 25 percent of it if he could find it. Hurkos walked back and forth across the garden many times but didn't find any gold. Suddenly he felt "pulled" toward a small greenhouse. Bursting into it, he began spilling plants onto the ground. The gardener tried to stop him, but when Hurkos upended yet another flower box, out fell the missing tin box, full of gold. The gardener confessed that he had found the box and had been planning to make off with it. Hurkos had solved the case but his psychic powers were not perfect. He did not get the promised 25 percent. The owner of the gold blandly informed Hurkos that there was no written contract between them.

3. Harold Lothridge. The body of five-year-old Dorothy Schneider was found in the bushes near a country lane outside Mount Morris, Michigan, on January 12, 1928. She had last been seen getting into a blue sedan, but there were no further clues. About a week after the discovery of the body, a twenty-five-year-old carpenter, Harold Lothridge, woke up at two o'clock in the morning, screaming and bathed in sweat. His wife tried to calm him. "That child," he gasped. "That poor little girl who was murdered near Mount Morris last week. My God, it's terrible."

"What is it?" his wife asked.

Lothridge shuddered. "I dreamed I was somewhere near when the car drove up. I saw the man who killed her. I could hear the little girl crying. She kept saying, 'I want to go home. I want to go home.'" Lothridge hesitated, as though debating whether to tell his wife more. "The terrible thing is both of us know the killer very well. It was Adolph Hotelling."

The couple slept no more that night and the next day, Lothridge went to talk to his father. Lothridge had no reputation as a psychic. His father heard him out and told him to be quiet about it, that he couldn't go around accusing Adolph Hotelling of killing little girls just because of a nightmare. Things were now out of Lothridge's control, however. Two fellow carpenters had overheard the conversation between father and son, and notified the sheriff's office that the pair knew something about the Schneider murder.

When Harold Lothridge was interviewed, the two deputies who questioned him were let down when they heard he had merely had a dream. Still, they were assigned to investigate the lead and they did. They drove out to Hotelling's home to question him. Hotelling told them he had been home alone at the time of the girl's abduction. The officers then asked him if his car was blue. He told them it was black and invited them to see for themselves. He showed them a black sedan in the garage. The officers, satisfied, were about to leave when one of them noticed a scratch on the car fender where some black paint had been scraped off. There was blue paint under it. He scraped more black paint off with his ring.

Hotelling broke down then and confessed. He had killed the child and had committed many other crimes. He had been having nightmares since the murder. He sobbed, "That little girl comes back to me every night. She keeps crying, 'I want to go home,' over and over again."

Caught because of Harold Lothridge's dream, Hotelling was sentenced to life imprisonment.

4. Arthur P. Roberts. On October, 18, 1935, Arthur Price Roberts visited the Milwaukee police and warned them that the city was in for a rash of terrorist bombings. "I see two banks blown up and perhaps the city hall. Going to blow up the police stations." The Milwaukee police did not sneer at Roberts. He had a reputation as a psychic and had been solving crimes since the turn of the century. The police beefed up patrols. On October 26 the village hall in suburban Horewood was destroyed by a dynamite blast that killed two children and injured dozens of people. The next day, two Milwaukee banks were dynamited. Later that same day, two police stations were rocked by bombs. Police asked Roberts where the next bombing would occur and he told them there would be a big one south of the Menominee River "and that'll be all." It was comforting to police that this would be the last bombing but they were determined to try to stop it. Police flooded the Menominee district, but they found nothing in time.

On Sunday afternoon, November 4, the area was hit by a huge explosion that was heard eight miles away. Ground zero turned out to be a garage that had been demolished. Human flesh was picked up in bits and pieces for blocks around. Were they more victims of the bombers or were they the mad bombers themselves? It took patient scientific police work to answer the question. The two dead men found were Hugh Rutkowski, aged twenty-one, and Paul Chovonee, aged nineteen. They had been in the process of putting together their sixth bomb when fifty pounds of dynamite somehow exploded. The full story of Roberts' predictions, reported in the Milwaukee *News* of November 6, 1935, had been true in every detail.

5. Maximillian Langsner. It was a duel of minds that was to last five hours. Inside the prison cell was a pasty-faced black-haired young man who alternately sat sullenly or paced nervously back and forth. Outside the cell sat a dapper little man with a waxed mustache, resting his chin on a gold-headed cane. For the first hour the prisoner tried to ignore the odd-looking man. By the second hour he was cursing under his breath. By the third hour he was snarling for the man to go away. The strange visitor was a well-known mentalist named Maximillian Langsner, who had been performing in Vancouver, Canada. Langsner had been summoned to provincial police headquarters at Edmonton, where an investigation was under way of a mass killing in the farming community of Mannville, Alberta.

In 1928 the Royal Canadian Mounted Police were summoned to the Booher farm, where they found Mrs. Henry Booher, her son Fred, and two farmhands shot to death. They had been shot with a .303 rifle, which couldn't be found. The police had a theory, however. They suspected that the Boohers' younger son, Vernon, had killed his mother, and because his brother had witnessed it, Vernon had shot Fred as well. Then Vernon had to shoot the two hired hands because they had seen him kill Fred. They clapped Vernon Booher into jail; but he wouldn't talk, nor would he say where the murder weapon was. Without that, they had no case.

That was when Inspector Hancock happened to read a newspaper report about mind reader Langsner. He felt that nothing would be lost by trying Langsner and invited him. When the Vienna-born mind reader arrived, he insisted he had to sit in Vernon Booher's presence until, as he put it, the young man's brain started giving off impulses. Langsner said Vernon would know he wanted to determine where the rifle was and so would start thinking about it and give off the proper impulses. Finally, after five hours, Langsner got up and left. He had what he wanted to know.

Langsner sketched a farmhouse, several bushes, and some trees. Then he sketched more bushes, some 500 yards from the house, and said the rifle was buried there. Langsner described the house as white with red shutters—the Booher house. When Langsner and the police went to the house, they had no trouble finding the bushes that Langsner had drawn. It took only a few minutes of exploring to find some soft earth. Soon a .303 Enfield was discovered. Brought to the farm and confronted with the rifle, Vernon Booher confessed to the murders, and the scenario was exactly as the police had theorized. But it had all depended on a mentalist, Maximillian Langsner, to "read" the clues that trapped the suspect.

6. Abraham Lincoln. Though America's president during the Civil War did not solve his own murder, he did dream about it. Three days before his assassination, Lincoln told his wife, a presidential aide, and two friends about a dream that was haunting him:

"About ten days ago I retired very late. I had been up waiting for important dispatches from the front. I could not have been long in bed when I fell into a slumber, for I was weary. I soon began to dream. There seemed to be a deathlike stillness about me. Then I heard subdued sobs, as if a number of people were weeping. I thought I left my bed and wandered downstairs. There the silence was broken by some pitiful sobbing, but the mourners were invisible. I went from room to room; no living person was in sight, but the same mournful sounds of distress met me as I passed along. It was light in all the rooms; every object was familiar to me; but where were all the people who were grieving as if their hearts would break? I was puzzled and alarmed. What could be the meaning of all this? Determined to find the cause of a state of things so mysterious and shocking, I kept on until I arrived at the East Room, which I entered. There I met with a sickening surprise. Before me was a catafalque, on which rested a corpse wrapped in funeral vestments. Around it were stationed soldiers who were acting as guards; and there was a throng of people, some gazing mournfully upon the corpse, whose face was covered, others weeping pitifully. 'Who is dead in the White House?' I demanded of one of the soldiers. 'The President,' was his answer; 'he was killed by an assassin!' Then came a loud burst of grief from the crowd, which awoke me from my dream. I slept no more that night; and although it was only a dream, I have been strangely annoyed by it ever since."

Later that night, the presidential aide, Colonel Ward H. Lamon, wrote down Lincoln's words of prophecy.

Seven Strange Solutions

1. The Dead Do Talk. New York City homicide detectives still talk about the murder case in which a dead man spoke to catch his murderer. One night in 1941, police responded to an emergency call about a shooting in a married couple's apartment. The husband had been shot and killed. Both the wife and the other woman, a houseguest, insisted they had been sleeping and were awakened by shots but knew nothing else. The appearance of the apartment pointed very much to an "inside job," however, since the victim had been shot with his own revolver, which was found lying on a table in the next room. It had been wiped clean of all fingerprints. Much of the furniture had been overturned, indicating a fight, which probably would have awakened the women.

Highly doubtful of the story they were getting from the women, detectives kept pounding them with questions until dawn, trying to trip them up. Then a very strange thing happened. The dead man, lying on the floor of the apartment, suddenly seemed to groan several times. It unnerved both the women and the detectives; only the medical examiner on the scene realized what was happening but prudently remained silent. Meanwhile, the wife could stand it no longer and started blurting out a confession. She had hated her husband and shot him. Now he was seemingly accusing her after his own death. What had really happened? Occasionally, the stomach muscles contract before the onset of rigor mortis. This contraction forces gas up the esophagus and against the vocal cords, producing strange "talking" sounds.

2. Kiss of Guilt. In a hit-and-run case in a western U.S. city recently, a young man was hit not by one but by two cars. The first car struck him a glancing blow that threw him in front of a second car, which then killed him. The driver of the first car fled but the driver of the second car remained at the scene. This driver was cleared of blame even though his car had done the fatal damage. A search was launched for sedans that fit the description of the first car. Several were located but none was dented, which is generally the case when a car strikes a body with only a glancing blow. Thus there were no paint chips on the body to match up with car paint. The police soon made an arrest, however. Dusting of each car produced a perfect set of prints of the victim on the suspected car. They were not fingerprints but, rather, "lip prints." Since the dead youth had not known the driver of the first car, the only time he could have "kissed" the auto was during the accident.

3. Delivered in Chains. One of the strangest endings of a murder hunt occurred in Baghdad in 1864. Aboard a ship bound for Baghdad, sailors slipped chains on one of their comrades while he was sleeping. They kept him in chains until they had almost reached port and then discovered they had lost the key to the chain locks. Once they were in port, a blacksmith was summoned, but he refused to remove the irons without a magistrate's order, for fear he would be charged with helping a lawbreaker escape. The sailor was brought to court, where a magistrate heard the story and ordered his release. As the sailor was being ushered through the streets to the blacksmith's shop to have his chains removed, he attracted a large, laughing crowd. Suddenly a man pushed his way through the crowd, screaming, "That is the villain! That is the man who murdered my brother two years ago and fled!" Still in chains, the sailor was led back to the magistrate. The murder charge was investigated and found to be accurate. All because of a seafaring hoax, a killer was caught, tried, and executed.

4. Second Chance. Johnny Cordes, one of New York City's most fabled detectives, had the ability to sense the solution to a crime. Once, the body of a woman was found hanging from a chandelier. The death was classified as a suicide, but Cordes instinctively thought differently and got the name of the woman's boyfriend from her landlady. He located the man a few hours later at a picnic on Long Island and walked up to him and said, "You're wanted for assault, Joe. You're lucky the rope broke and that she's alive. Otherwise you'd be held for murder." Joe was much relieved and blurted out a confession that he had beaten his inamorata and hanged her.

The confession that was tricked out of the killer put him in the electric chair.

5. The Great Fingerprint Hunt. A murder in England was solved because of a promise Scotland Yard made to the public. On May 15, 1948, early in the morning, an intruder slipped into the children's ward of the Queen's Park Hospital in Blackburn and kidnapped a four-year-old girl. Outside, on the grounds of the hospital, he assaulted her and then killed her. Bloodhounds failed to pick up the murderer's trail and police were left with just one tangible clue, the culprit's fingerprints, which he had left on a bottle on a table by the child's bed. Unfortunately, there was no record of this set of prints, and no logical suspect turned up who matched the prints. Thereupon, Scotland Yard announced it was "requesting" that all of the 48,000 males in the area over the age of fifteen be fingerprinted. House-to-house gathering of prints went on for a quarter of a year before the killer was finally fingerprinted and arrested. By that time 45,000 sets of prints had been taken. Then, in accordance with the pledge Scotland Yard had made, the police publicly destroyed all the prints they had collected.

6. The Sealed Bathroom. New York City detectives who answered a death-by-stabbing call were perplexed, thinking they had on their hands a strange, sealed-room case more suited to the movies than to real life. A man was found stabbed through the heart in a third-floor bathroom that was locked on the inside. There was one window in the bathroom, but it had been painted shut and had not been opened. The death would have been put down as suicide except for one troublesome detail: *There was no knife!* Though this was a perplexing problem to the detectives, it wasn't to the physician from the medical examiner's office. "Never mind what happened here," he told them. "See if you can find out about a knife fight anywhere in the area nearby." The police checked and found there had been and that the victim had been stabbed. As the doctor explained later, it was entirely possible for a man stabbed in the heart to walk a block from a fight, climb two flights of stairs, lock himself in a bathroom, and then finally collapse. Such victims often head for the bathroom to clean themselves up.

7. The Poisoning of Napoleon. One hundred and forty-one years after the death of Napoleon in 1821, three scientists—two Swedes and a Scot—obtained a lock of his hair. It had been clipped by Napoleon's valet after the emperor died on St. Helena. After the passage of more than 140 years the three scientists were able to check on the presence of arsenic in the hair—thanks to a special property of arsenic. It is indestructible. They measured ten parts of arsenic in a million, which is much greater than the normal amount. Then the scientists measured the amounts of arsenic at different points on a strand, which was some five inches long. The amounts of arsenic varied, from which fact the scientists were able to deduce that the great military genius had been getting regular doses of arsenic for about four months before he died. They published their findings in the English scientific journal *Nature* and concluded that they were in agreement with Napoleon, who had believed he was being poisoned. Two months before he died, Napoleon wrote, "I am dying before my time, murdered by the English oligarchy and its hired assassin."

The scientists concluded that Napoleon had been poisoned by his jailers. While little scientific objection could be made to their findings that Napoleon had been poisoned, their conclusions in detection were still open to question. It was possible that the jailers were not involved, that Napoleon had been murdered instead by Sir Hudson Lowe, the governor of St. Helena, who has often been accused of having mistreated Napoleon. Then, too, there were Napoleon's French attendants, all supposedly devoted, but could they have been paid by certain parties in France who wanted to ensure that Napoleon would never return? And then there was Napoleon himself. In despair, he could conceivably have decided to poison himself and at the same time incriminate the hated English. Napoleon was undoubtedly poisoned, but there is insufficient evidence to date to identify the poisoner with any certainty.

Five Real-Life Cases for Sherlock Holmes

"Sir Arthur Conan Doyle," said Sir Basil Thomson, one-time head of Scotland Yard, "would have made an outstanding detective had he devoted himself to crime detection rather than authorship. There was much of Holmes in Doyle." With armchair logic, Doyle solved some of Britain's most heinous murder cases, freed innocent men who were in jail, and, in that country's greatest criminal cause *célèbre*, freed a man, who had been sentenced to the gallows for a murder he did not commit. Here are five from Sir Arthur's casebook.

1. The Brides in the Bath. Long before George Joseph Smith, the notorious lady killer, was caught for drowning his wives in a bathtub, Doyle had spotted the murder technique. Doyle was an avid newspaper reader, especially of the sensation-minded British Sunday papers, and when in 1913 he read an item about the tragic death of a bride, Alice Burnham Smith, of Blackpool, in Lancashire, his interest was instantly aroused. According to the newspaper, she had apparently suffered an attack of epilepsy, then fainted and drowned. Doyle clipped the item as a sample of a probable murder. Then, a year later, he found a story about Margaret Elizabeth Lofty Lloyd drowning in her bathtub. Now the Sherlock Holmes in Doyle could not rest. He hired a model and had her step into a filled bathtub. He told her to let her head and body sag to simulate unconsciousness. He had her do this over and over. But no matter in what normal position she started, the girl was unable to slump in a way that would submerge her head. It was necessary for Sir Arthur to grab the girl by the ankles and pull her legs over the edge of the tub and then shove her head under the water before she could be in a drowning position. Excited by his findings,

Doyle rushed to a friend, Inspector John Neil of Scotland Yard. Eventually, Smith was arrested and Doyle's experiment was repeated in court by the prosecution. Smith was found guilty and hanged.

2. The Body in the Moat.

A reporter for the London *Times* interviewed Doyle to get his comments on famous murder cases. One case in particular interested the reporter because he had covered it. It involved the disappearance of a wealthy woman, Camille Cecile Holland. Her fortune had been systematically siphoned off by a swindler, Captain Samuel Dougal. For a time Dougal and Miss Holland both disappeared. Dougal was found by police, who also uncovered proof that he had forged Miss Holland's name to various documents. But that was not proof of murder and Dougal insisted that Miss Holland had told him she was going on an extended holiday on the Continent.

"Naturally, the police searched all of Moat Farm, Miss Holland's home, but found no body," the reporter told Doyle. "They went over the barn and the cellar and virtually tore the house down looking for her."

Doyle sucked on his pipe thoughtfully. "And did they search the moat?"

"Moat? What moat?" (The reporter made a perfect Watson.)

"The name of the farm," Sir Arthur said. "Moat Farm. I presume there was a moat."

"Oh, that." The reporter shrugged. "There had been one, but it had been filled in by the previous owner when he sold the property to Miss Holland."

"And was that ground dug up?"

"No, it wasn't. No one ever thought of that."

"It's rather obvious, then," Sir Arthur said. "I would suggest searching all the ground filling the moat, since, if the earth hadn't been there very long, it would have been comparatively soft. Thus, if the killer got it into his head to bury the body, he might have thought he could do so in relative safety, since the soft ground from digging would arouse no particular suspicion."

The following night, by the light of torches, the body of Camille Cecile Holland was dug up from a filled-in spot in the old moat, at the rear of the house. She had been shot through the head.

Sir Arthur had solved the case without leaving his study.

Years later, Doyle gave credit for helping solve the case to another writer, Edgar Allan Poe, pointing out that the classic plot Poe related in "The Purloined Letter" was what had brought the solution so readily to mind. In that story an important letter had been hidden in the one place no one would look for it—right out in the open on a desk.

3. Hunt for a Slaughterer. George Edalji of Wyrley had been given seven years' imprisonment for the sadistic slaying of scores of farm animals. The acts had apparently sprung from the killer's awful desire to watch horses, cattle, and sheep bleed to death. Sir Arthur became interested in the case because he was struck by the shocking weakness of the evidence against Edalji. The killer had left prints of run-down heels near the scene of his last crime. In addition, the killer had been observed fleeing the scene in a heavy rainstorm, and two witnesses had identified him as Edalji. There had been an anonymous letter blaming Edalji for the killings. Three years after Edalji went to prison, Doyle went to visit him. The man protested his innocence. What impressed Doyle most was that Edalji wore very thick glasses. He was blind as a bat without them. Could he have run so fast through a rainstorm with blurred vision? Doyle went to Wyrley and soon noted that in that poor community most men had heels that were very run-down. Doyle visited the scene of the last crime and reasoned that if the killer had run in the direction he had, he was probably fleeing toward his home. Edalji's home had been in that direction, so Doyle reasoned that the witnesses, their vision obstructed by the rain, had assumed the man was Edalji. Doyle soon found a man named Lewis living in the same direction and with a build similar to the convicted man's. Doyle observed him for several days and noticed he wore shoes with run-down heels. Doyle used a ruse to visit Lewis' barn and found a horse lancet, which was the sort of weapon the killer had used. He also learned that Lewis left the community for long stretches at a time. When he was gone, there were no animal killings. And Lewis' handwriting matched that of the anonymous letter. Could Lewis have written it to shift suspicion from himself?

Armed with all this evidence, Sir Arthur went to the police and demanded they begin an inquiry. The police refused. They did not want a fiction writer telling them how to do their work. "Never in all my life had I witnessed such an act of smallness," Doyle wrote later. He was not deterred, however. He wrote a series of articles about the case for the *Daily Telegraph*. When they started to appear, Lewis fled. Then an official investigation was launched and George Edalji was cleared.

4. The Man Who Was Almost Hanged. Doyle once received a letter from a convict in Peterhead Prison begging the author to come visit him and establish his innocence. The man was Oscar Slater, who had been sentenced to death for the murder of Marion Gilchrist, an eighty-two-year-old Glasgow spinster. At the last minute, Slater, a small, German man of thirty, had his sentence commuted to life imprisonment. He had been identified, after considerable hesitation, by two witnesses who had seen the murderer fleeing the dead woman's flat. Slater was caught a week later after he had pawned a brooch for about $250. The dead woman's servant identified the brooch as one that *could* have belonged to Miss Gilchrist. What most disturbed Sir Arthur about the police theory in the case was that Slater had allegedly stolen only the brooch out of Miss Gilchrist's jewel box, which had contained some $15,000 worth of valuables. Doyle reasoned that a killer, if he had time to find the jewel box, would have taken all or nothing. And Slater claimed the brooch was an old family heirloom that he had pawned many times before.

Doyle plunged into the case and discovered that the police had dug up many details that had been suppressed because they could not be tied to Slater. The killer had worn a gray coat and a dark cap and there was no evidence that Slater had ever worn a cap in his life. The point had been quietly forgotten. Then Doyle produced his best bit of evidence: witnesses who had seen Slater with the brooch in question weeks before the killing. In 1914, after Sir Arthur had worked on the case for six years, a hearing was held, but because the police theory had not been totally disproved, the decision went against Slater. Sir Arthur continued to search for more evidence. It took him another fourteen years to finally prove Slater's total innocence. In 1928 Slater was given a full and unconditional pardon and a cash reward of about $30,000.

5. The Lady Forger. When Sir Arthur cleared Oscar Slater, he was in the twilight of his years and thought it was going to be his last real-life case. Shortly before his death in 1930, however, he interested himself in the case of a young woman who was accused of bilking several storeowners out of large sums of money with bad checks. He had just begun investigating the case when he died. But six months later, another woman was arrested and confessed to the crimes for which the first woman had been convicted. Sir Arthur Conan Doyle, a detective the equal of his own Sherlock Holmes, again had been proved right in judging his fellowman.

VI.
UNDERWORLD VIGNETTES

Underworld Vignette #1

Dion O'Banion, who ruled Chicago's North Side after the First World War until he was shot and killed by the Capone mob in his flower shop in November 1924, was a strange mixture of ruthlessness, devoutness, and bigheartedness. "Deanie" started his criminal career as an enforcer for William Randolph Hearst's *Herald Examiner*, making sure newsstands understood the merits of taking the Hearst paper instead of others. Deanie went on to safecracking, bootlegging, and murder. His devoutness, however, did not permit him to go into the brothel racket, and not a single bordello ever appeared on O'Banion's North Side turf. If there was anything Deanie was really proud of, it was his big heart. He was always sending gifts to and paying the medical bills for citizens he shot down in error.

Underworld Vignette #2

Vito Genovese, the Mafia don who until his death in 1969 continued to direct criminal activities from his federal-prison cell after being sentenced to fifteen years, always exhibited the ability to adapt. Facing a murder charge in 1937, Genovese fled to Italy. In 1944 he wrangled an interpreter's job with U.S. Military Intelligence. Thanks to his efforts, the army was able to uncover a number of black-market operatives in southern Italy. Embarrassed authorities later discovered, however, that after Genovese denounced the black marketeers, he simply took over running their operations.

Underworld Vignette #3

Probably the clown prince of crimedom was Greasy Thumb Guzik, the bookkeeping brain of the Chicago syndicate. Guzik got his big start in criminality because Al Capone cottoned to him and liked to have a court jester around. The scene of many of Guzik's hijinks was the Four Deuces, the famous four-story pride and joy of Scarface Al Capone on Chicago's South Wabash Avenue. On the first floor was a bar, on the second and third were gambling joints, and on the fourth a remarkable bordello.

The Four Deuces was not without competition, especially from the Frolics Café nearby, which insisted on dispensing booze and women at cut-rate prices. When one of several murders occurred in the Four Deuces, Guzik had an inspiration of what to do with the body. He had it lugged to the Frolics and stuffed into the furnace. Then, playing the role of an irate citizen, Guzik telephoned police headquarters and protested that the Frolics was running an illegal crematorium without an undertaker's license. After the law found the body, they padlocked the joint and ripped up the premises looking for more corpses. They didn't find any or solve the mystery of the one in the furnace, but the Frolics never reopened.

Underworld Vignette #4

A gangster named Joseph Aiello was the leader of an Italian gang in Chicago that arose after the downfall of the Genna gang. For years Joey had tried to wrest control of

Unione Siciliana from Al Capone and, failing this, allied himself with Bugs Moran. He went on trying to knock off Capone, once by bribing a restaurant chef to put prussic acid in Capone's soup and once by putting a reward of $50,000 on his head. It was just as clear that Capone wanted Aiello dead, in fact, very dead. Thus when Aiello was cut down in a burst of machine-gun fire as he stepped onto the street from an apartment house on North Kolmar on October 23, 1930, he was killed in a way that represented the "full weight" of the Capone mob. Fifty-nine bullets were dug out of Aiello's body, with all the lead weighing more than a pound.

Underworld Vignette #5

The plight of the Mafia wife has been described as extremely comfortable in some cases and not very nice in others. When the relationship is a happy one, one cardinal rule seems to be followed: The wife pointedly knows absolutely nothing about what her husband does. When she does learn something, the circumstances can change radically. The wives of Mike Coppola are a case in point. Coppola inherited the New York rackets of Vito Genovese when the latter fled to Italy to escape a murder rap. (Coppola is said to have netted something like a million dollars a year from these rackets until the return of Genovese.) Coppola killed his first wife, Doris, after she had had the misfortune of hearing Coppola plan the murder of a New York politician. Mrs. Coppola died the day after she gave birth to a baby girl. It was the second Mrs. Coppola who finally accused him publicly of having done in her predecessor. She had been so mentally and physically abused by her husband that she finally testified against him. The following year, she committed suicide.

Underworld Vignette #6

Big Jim O'Leary, the son of the Mrs. O'Leary of cow fame, died a millionaire in 1926 thanks to his gambling operations. Big Jim always stated proudly that his famed "gambling emporium on Halsted Street in Chicago was "fireproof, bomb-proof, and police-proof." The place was undented in the gambling wars of 1907. The police did occasionally breach Big Jim's security system, but he usually was ready for them. Once, when a mob of police broke into the place, they found it bare save for a plain table at which an old man was devoutly reading a Bible. Another time, O'Leary primed his inner walls with red pepper; when the police wielded their axes into the zinc, they were blinded temporarily so that most required hospitalization and several were unable to return to duty for a week.

Underworld Vignette #7

Chicago's notorious Whiskey Row, in the Gay Nineties was known as the surest place in the Windy City for a man to be robbed, maimed, or murdered. The worst dive in the area was the Lone Star Saloon and Palm Garden, run by a tough, mean barman named Mickey Finn. For a long time Finn, who used girls as part of his operation, restricted his activities to pickpocketing and rolling an occasional drunk. Then, in 1898, he bought a recipe from a black voodoo doctor and went into high gear with the illicit activities that would make "Mickey Finn" a phrase in the dictionary.

Finn developed the Mickey Finn Special, which was a compound of raw alcohol, water, and a secret voodoo mixture. Finn's girls were ordered to push the drink on any lone customer. Once a victim drank the brew, he would get talkative, walk around in a restless manner, and then fall into a deep sleep from which he could not be roused until the effects wore off, several hours later. The victim would be hauled into a back room, which Finn called his "operating room," where the actual robbing was done. For some reason Finn would don a derby hat and a clean white apron when he and his wife were busy at their task. The victim was stripped to the skin to see if he wore a money belt, and then every stitch of clothing was searched for valuables. If the drugged man's clothing was of value, they too were kept and he was dressed in old castoffs. The victim would then be dumped in a nearby alley. When he awoke, he seldom remembered what had happened. Eventually, the law got onto Finn and his license was revoked. It was the worst thing that could have happened. Finn then sold the secret of his recipe to a half-dozen eager saloonkeepers and soon the Mickey Finn was in use all over America.

Underworld Vignette #8

Back in the days when Norway was more Norse than Christian, criminals developed an unusual way of breaking into Christian homes during the Yuletide season. They would gather in front of the house and sing Christmas carols. When the occupants opened the door to wish the carolers well, they would immediately be pounced upon and killed, and their houses looted. The tactic has remained a worldwide underworld ruse ever since. It was used during a recent Christmas in the Philippines by bandits who killed several dozen victims.

VII.
WOMEN'S WORLD

J. Edgar Hoover's Seven Nastiest Women

Way back when it was still considered ungallant to attribute the ills and failings of men to women as well, the FBI's J. Edgar Hoover went one giant step further and announced, "Women are deadlier." He cited female mass murderers who have never gotten their proper acclaim, mothers who trained their broods in crime, and molls who bossed their men. Here are some of them.

1. Two Unheralded Lethal Ladies. Madame Van der Linden, the Leiden poisoner, busied herself between 1869 and 1885 with the prodigious task of doing away with 102 people. She is officially credited with polishing off twenty-seven, and she made another twoscore very ill.

Helen Jegado of France, another poisoner, trailed Madame Van der Linden by only one victim. She killed twenty-six people but is known to have tried to finish off another dozen or so.

2. Two Awful Moms. Ma Barker, of course. Ma, her sons Arthur "Doc" and Freddie, and Alvin "Creepy" Karpis were the nucleus of the Barker gang. Ma did the thinking and the boys the executing. The police tried to run down the mob through Ma with *cherchez l'homme*. Bored by her husband— he was too honest, too slow—Ma found love in her glamorous middle age in the form of a romantic bill poster named Arthur Dunlop. Unfortunately for poor Arthur, right after he joined the crime clan, the gang began having some close scrapes with the law. The suspicion grew that Arthur was a "squealer."

Ma had to choose between love and crime. Arthur's bullet-ripped body turned up near a Wisconsin lake. The only clue to his killer was a woman's blood-soaked glove lying near the corpse.

Ma could have decided to get rid of Dunlop for other reasons. Jealousy might have been a factor. She was bitterly jealous of the gun molls her boys picked up, and she never allowed these women under her roof. The gang members could drink liquor only when Ma didn't see. She often lectured them that drink loosened the tongue.

Ma looked upon crime as strictly business. When planning a bank job, she would make the boys memorize the "getaway chart." After preparing the map, she would drive around all the surrounding roads, tracking each turn and recording the speed and the exact mileage. She ran tests on both wet and dry roads. During an actual robbery, however, Ma would become a mother again, weeping hysterically for fear that something might happen to one of her brood.

Ma switched the gang from robbery to kidnapping because the former was often dangerous and the latter more lucrative. In 1933 the gang got $100,000 for the return of William A. Hamm, Jr., a St. Paul, Minnesota, brewer, and later $200,000 from the family of Edward George Bremer, a St. Paul banker.

But the end was near for the mob. A fingerprint found in the Bremer snatch put the heat on. Son Freddie and Alvin Karpis underwent plastic surgery to alter their faces and fingerprints but succeeded only in enduring a lot of pain. Karpis left the gang. Son Doc was arrested in Chicago and sent to Alcatraz, where he later died attempting to shoot his way out. Meanwhile, the FBI traced Ma and her favorite son, Freddie, to a Florida cottage. When they called on the pair to come out and surrender, Ma jammed a machine gun through a window and let loose a hail of bullets. After a six-hour gunfight, during which 1,500 bullets hit the hideout, Ma and Freddie were dead. Freddie had eleven bullets in one shoulder and three in his head. Ma fell while still holding her machine gun. One shot had killed her.

Shoebox Annie French. Annie has been compared to the witches in the more gruesome versions of some fairy tales. She earned her nickname through the shoplifting technique of heisting merchandise with a trick shoebox. She and her son, William, worked as a criminal team in the Northwest. Two persons who entered Shoebox Annie's home were never seen again—at least not in one piece. Four others vanished. Ole Larson entered Annie's home in Anaconda, Montana, carrying a $750 draft. Ole was never seen again. Annie cashed the draft by forging the endorsement. Shortly thereafter, one of her son's lovers crossed the threshold of the house and vanished. A woman's bones were found later near Butte, but no identification could be made. Hoover credited Annie with being an expert at disposing of corpses, her infamous little shoebox apparently often carried items more gruesome than shoplifted goods.

But Annie was still a mother. Whenever William was doing time, she sent her son comforting letters saying she would pray he would find the right path when he got out. Annie indulged his taste for music by sending him a harmonica and a saxophone. She remained the indulgent mother when both were jailed by the State of Washington for killing a young naval officer, Jame E. Bassett. Bassett went to Annie's to sell his car. He was killed with a hammer and his body was dismembered. Time again for the shoebox.

Later, Annie confessed when she was informed that her son was talking. "I don't see why you are making such a fuss over this," she said. "My son needed an automobile. He had to murder Bassett to get it. . . . He was a nice boy, kind and gentle to his mother . . . and his victim never suffered."

3. Two Tough Molls. Some molls were more than molls, becoming, like Ma Barker, the brains behind their men. No one ever should have considered George "Machine Gun" Kelly as anything more than a good-natured slob, or, as he has also been described, "a bootlegger who spilled more than he delivered."

In 1927, however, George Kelly married Kathryn Shannon, a Texas widow with underworld connections. Vivacious and attractive, she was also ambitious—for George. Kelly had been a machine gunner in World War I, and as a wedding present his bride bought him a shiny machine gun. She made him practice shooting nuts off fence posts. Kathryn should have gone into advertising or public relations; she knew how to package her product. She would distribute spent cartridge cases in underworld dives, saying, "Have a souvenir of my husband, Machine Gun Kelly."

Eventually the underworld began to think there was something to Machine Gun Kelly, and he was recruited into a bank-robbery mob. George took part in robbing banks in Tupelo, Mississippi, and in Wilmer, Texas, both bush-league jobs. George would probably have been happy to stay small, but Kathryn wouldn't permit this. In 1933 Kathryn came up with a really ambitious project—kidnapping oil millionaire Charles Urschel. It was a job that bore the Machine Gun Kelly imprint, with any number of botches and glaring clues left behind. Somehow the gang collected the ransom and released their victim. But the FBI discovered the identities of all the culprits and, one by one, the gang was captured. Kathryn's idea of hiding out was wearing a red wig. In chasing gangland women, the FBI learned that any brunette or blonde fugitive could be counted on to become a redhead. Kathryn's new hair helped the FBI locate the Kellys in a Memphis hideout. Under the bed was her red wig, which since then has been on display at FBI headquarters in Washington, D. C.

In many ways, Vivian Chase was the toughest gun moll of the 1930s. She is considered to have been the chief planner and perpetrator of the August Luer kidnapping in Alton, Illinois. Six members of the gang were rounded up, but Vivian Chase eluded capture for the rest of her life—for two short years. One Sunday morning, a passerby discovered her body in an abandoned car behind a Kansas City Hospital. The FBI never found her killers or established a motive, but the genral word in the underworld was that Vivian had joined another gang and had sealed her doom by trying to take over.

4. The Naughtiest Con Lady. Avanna Sherrill had at least ninety other aliases, ranging all the way from aristocratic ones like Carolyn Ann Ardmore to more pedestrian ones like just plain Goofy. According to Hoover, women schemers were no match for men at planning a confidence scheme, but the ladies could always win out at improvisations. A genuine mistress of instant invention, Avanna scattered $1.25 million in worthless checks around the country. She was also a master criminal at stealing cars, often getting passersby to help her get her car started. Once, a man with whom she rode to Colorado offered to marry her and she accepted. She gave him a $1,600 phony check, which she said was insurance money for flood losses, and took from him $1,200 in cash and his automobile. She left him waiting in a theatre lobby. "As far as I know," she said to the FBI after she was arrested, "he is still in the theater."

Four Notorious Women Comment on Their Conviction

1. Patty Hearst, who entered American folklore by being kidnapped in her nightclothes by a group of terrorists led by a half-crazed escaped convict: "I wonder if I ever had a chance."

2. Alice Crimmins, charged with the murder of her two young children, on hearing the jury's verdict: "Oh, my God, how could they do it?"

3. Lynette "Squeaky" Fromme, convicted of attempting to kill President Gerald Ford: "I can't be rehabilitated because I haven't done anything wrong. . . . I want a world at peace. I know no one can bring it. You only have ten years of air and water."

4. Sara Jane Moore, also convicted of attempting to kill Gerald Ford: "Am I sorry I tried? Yes, because it accomplished little except to throw away the rest of my life. And, no, I'm not sorry I tried, because at the time it seemed a correct expression of my anger, and, if successful, the assassination, combined with the public disclosures of this government's own activities in this area, just might have triggered the kind of chaos that could have started the upheaval of change."

Five Shady Ladies

In the area of great flimflams and frauds, women can be audacious, sometimes capitalizing on their special assets, at other times matching, dollar for dollar, the amounts that men have been able to gouge out of a gullible public.

1. Mary Toft, The Rabbit Girl. In 1726, in Goldalming, England, a girl named Mary Toft told an incredible story. She said she had given birth to twelve rabbits. Remarkably, her doctor concurred with her story. It was, of course, an incredible fraud on Mary's part, one that her doctor was not party to. She had actually conned him into believing her tale. When the amazed physician made the story public, it swept all of Britain. Almost everyone believed the story, especially after two leading doctors investigated and agreed that Mary's claim was valid. Mary became an instant celebrity. Incredible bids were made to buy the rabbits or just to view them. Then, because the girl said she was soon to have more bunnies, she was taken to a London hospital. There, a royal physician, who was not prepared to buy the tale, ordered her kept under constant surveillance by nurses, day and night. Such precautions made it impossible for the girl to smuggle in any rabbits, and thus she could not work her trickery. The doctor issued a report denouncing the girl as a phony. The ensuing public hostility didn't die down until Mary was arrested and had confessed.

Shortly thereafter, a London magician performed a new trick for the first time, that of pulling a rabbit out of a hat. He had learned Mary's technique but applied it in a more sociably acceptable manner. At least Mary Toft would go down in history as the mother of the rabbit trick that for a time stumped the medical profession. A collection of works on the Mary Toft case can be found in the U.S. Army Medical Library in Washington, D.C.

2. Gold Brick Cassie. The greatest woman swindler in American history was a brassy beauty named Cassie Chadwick. At the turn of the last century, she concocted an amazing hoax that fooled the top legal and banking brains of Cleveland, Ohio. She convinced them that she was the illegitimate daughter of steel magnate Andrew Carnegie. It became the main subject whispered in polite Cleveland society. Cassie then deposited some $7 million in supposedly valid securities in a Cleveland bank, given to her she said, by her "father." She got a receipt for these securities and that, along with the fact that it was common knowledge that she was Carnegie's daughter, opened bank vaults around the country to her. No one dared mention any of this to Carnegie, who was just about the most imperious man in the country, one known for his vindictiveness and obviously not one to have a bastardy charge hurled in his face. Cassie started off borrowing small—in $50,000 lots. She paid the interest promptly and repaid the loan in full when necessary. Then she went whole hog, making huge loans and using other loans to pay the first loans back. Pretty soon, bankers came to her to lend her money.

Cassie traveled to Europe with her husband, a man from a Cleveland family that dripped respectability. Her husband, too, believed her Carnegie story. Cassie gave away a lot of money in the form of gifts and donations, but she borrowed a lot more. The bubble finally burst in late 1904. Cassie couldn't keep the money flow going while siphoning off so much for her own fun. Runs on banks developed in every city Cassie had ever visited. A bank president whose institution Cassie was into for $1.25 million keeled over with heart failure.

Newspapers dug up the fact that years earlier, Cassie had been arrested in Canada for small-time fraud, but her current actions were no longer small-time. It was estimated that she had bamboozled banks and private lenders out of something like $20 million. Many of Cassie's victims never stepped forward, probably fearing that they would be a laughingstock. Cassie was tried and sentenced to ten years in prison. She died there in 1907, in her forties, sickened by her confinement—but rich in memories.

3. Nothing Falsie. In a profession notorious for its phony gadgets, a well-known spiritualist, Mrs. Hannah Ross, came up with what must stand as the most bald-faced of all. She was the most popular medium in Boston in the 1880s because she could apparently cause a long-dead baby to materialize. Not only were the dumbfounded members of her audiences permitted to see the spirit; they were even allowed to kiss and pet it. Then a newspaperman and the police launched an investigation that spoiled the medium's good thing. There was a reason for the realism of the "baby spirit," which not only looked like a baby but felt like one. In a dark room, spiritualist Ross would seat herself in a cabinet and go into her trance. Then she would expose one of her breasts through a slit in the curtain surrounding her. On her breast she had painted the face of an infant child.

4. Ma Crime. In the last half of the 19th century Frederika "Marm" Mandelbaum was New York's queen of crime. The nation's most prosperous and daring "fence," she came to be the one-woman brain behind several gangs of bank robbers, burglars, blackmailers, and confidence men. Coming to America from Germany in 1849, Marm settled in a huge mansion in the Kleine Deutschland section of Manhattan. She quickly became a fence and her home became a "drop" for many small criminals. But Marm had bigger dreams and soon worked her way up, dealing in time with only the more proficient producers in the field of theft and larceny.

As her wealth grew, Marm, or the Widow Mandelbaum, began stepping up in society. She threw lavish parties in her mansion and mixed at her dinner table judges, lawyers, and politicians with burglars, bank robbers, and confidence men. Among the latter were Mark Shinburn, an elegant burglar, and George Leslie, an equally elegant bank robber, both of whom were suave and cultured and could hold their own with any society dame seated next to them. Marm used these social gatherings not only for her personal gratification but also as a way to find places to rob. When she learned that the owners of some classy home were going to be away, she sent her boys right over to strip the place clean, and that meant clean—including the paintings on the wall and even the wallpaper if it was of particular value.

Marm maintained several warehouses in Brooklyn where stolen goods were stored, their labels, trademarks, and other identifying features having been removed. They were then shipped out for resale as far away as Chicago. Whenever one of her boys was caught, Marm would see that he got off. Sometimes she could buy courtroom acquittals. Better yet, she could prevent the arrest of her boys. Policemen all over town were on her payroll, and she had so many spies at police headquarters that she could say she knew whenever one of the big brass felt like sneezing. When Marm couldn't prevent the arrest or conviction of one of her boys, she would buy a pardon at the going market rate or, failing that, arrange a jailbreak.

Though she was hardly a raving beauty, Frederika was lovingly regarded by the underworld. According to one Banjo Pete Emerson: "She had the more important beauty of the heart. She was scheming and dishonest as the day is long, but could be like an angel to the worst devil as long as he played square with her."

In some three-plus decades Marm is estimated to have handled something like $20 million in stolen goods—and this in nineteenth century dollars—and to have become a millionaire in her own right. The district attorney finally nailed Marm by hiring Pinkerton detectives to get evidence against her, and she was indicted in 1884. Marm managed to get out on bail and promptly skipped to Canada, from which she could not be extradited under a loophole in the law. She lived out her days there in comfort.

5. How Madame Humbert Conned France. There is a great similarity between Cassie Chadwick and Thérèse Humbert, and both made millions. But Madame Humbert lasted longer and was more daring. In 1878 Thérèse Daurignac kicked off her monumental swindle with fanfare, announcing to the press that she had been left $20 million by a grateful American millionaire, Robert H. Crawford. Thérèse, a young peasant girl, had nursed him through a very serious illness some years before. The fortune was in stocks and bonds, and would be sent to her shortly from the United States. That was enough to make Thérèse the toast of Paris. She was deluged with offers of credit and bank loans, at high interest rates, of course. Then she had two accomplices show up as Robert and Henry Crawford, the nephews of her late benefactor, with what they said was a later will, which left them half the estate and Thérèse the other half. They started a lawsuit and the courts ordered the securities sealed pending the outcome. Already a sensation, Thérèse capped everything by marrying Frédéric Humbert, the son of the minister of justice.

The cousins lost their suit and promptly appealed. They kept on appealing and appealing. Sometimes Thérèse would go to court against them, once, for example, to keep the cousins from annoying her. Through it all, bankers showered money on Thérèse, satisfied with their high interest rates and confident they would get their principal back "once the estate is settled." This went on for twenty-four years while Madame Humbert bought large estates, luxurious yachts, works of art, and valuable gems. It was not until 1902 that a creditor finally got suspicious and checked up on the late millionaire Crawford. He had never existed! The safe with the Crawford fortune was opened. It was found to contain a brick, a hairpin, and a thirty-centime note. There were at least ten suicides among her victims, who saw their financial institutions wrecked. Hundreds of others went into bankruptcy.

Meanwhile, Madame Humbert had disappeared. She was finally arrested in Spain, with her husband and her brothers— the Crawford nephews. For the second time in her life, Thérèse returned to France as a heroine. The press loved her for her magnificent hoax. Picture postcards of her were big sellers. Even with the huge sums involved in crime, Thérèse Humbert got only a five-year prison sentence and her husband and brothers got only three.

VIII.
PRACTICAL ADVICE FOR THE FRIGHTENED

Seven Anti-mugger Rules

The best rules on how to avoid being mugged come not from the police or other crime-prevention experts but from muggers themselves. It should be remembered that muggers work the meanest streets, and they also are potential victims of other muggers. It is for this reason that the advice of a reformed mugger, Tom "Baby Face" Ryan, has special meaning. He has an angelic face, and thus found it easy not to arouse suspicion in potential victims; at the same time, his looks invited attack by other street marauders. In his memoirs, he lists the following survival rules:

1. Always walk fast and with an air of self-confidence. This shows you are very sure of yourself and the mugger may think you are a cop, a decoy, or someone who is carrying a gun. The mugger doesn't need you. He can wait for Mr. Meek.

2. Walk in the middle of a dark street. The mugger's advantage of surprise is thus gone. Again, he may figure he is dealing with someone who's on the alert and perhaps very confident, a person too dangerous to try to take.

3. If you must venture on the streets at two o'clock in the morning, carry an umbrella, especially if it is not raining and has not rained for some time. Muggers traditionally regard an umbrella under such circumstances as an object for self-defense. They'll pass that person by. The next one may not have an umbrella.

4. Always walk defensively; that is, know where you intend to move in case you are threatened. Watch for lighted windows—in case of danger, run to it and yell out, "Help! I'm being followed." It doesn't matter if there is anybody at the

window or not. Muggers will seldom accept that kind of challenge as long as they can retreat into the shadows.

5. If you are a woman and feel you are threatened, run to the nearest mailbox and throw your purse in and scream as loud as you can. A mugger may not be bothered attacking you if he feels his loot is lost in any case.

6. Don't scream after a mugger grabs you. He'll instinctively try to silence you. But do scream before he has you, especially if you are a man. Muggers don't expect men to scream and it throws them off balance. Muggers function best when the element of surprise is in their favor.

7. If you are cornered and still have time to bluff, do so. Ryan tells of being cornered by another mugger and yelling out, "Tom, Bill, Jonesy, stakeout three. We got a mugger." Even Ryan was surprised at the mugger's response. He raised his arms and surrendered. "I told him to turn around, put his arms forward, and lean against the wall. Then I told him to bring one hand down and loosen his belt and let his pants drop. Cops order suspects to do that so they can't run away. As soon as he did that, I ran like hell."

Six Facts You Should Know About Burglaries

1. Between 50 and 60 percent of all burglaries do not involve forced entry; usually the homeowner has neglected to lock a door or window.

2. Fifty-four percent of all burglaries are the work of youths eighteen years old and younger.

3. There is a burglary committed every fifteen seconds.

4. Property loss from burglaries is greater than from any other crime.

5. Less than 15 percent of all property lost from burglaries is ever located by the police and returned to the owner.

6. Four out of five burglaries of private homes and apartments occur when nobody is home.

Eight Ways to Burglarproof Your Home

1. Surround your property with a combination fence and hedge, especially the thorny kind. An intruder will think twice about landing in a thicket of thorns.

2. Attach an electric alarm to your gate and activate it at night. This will warn you if a stranger enters, and when a potential burglar hears the sound, he generally loses interest in going any further.

3. Have an outside light that illuminates the front door. This light should be on all night and have a timer device that turns it off with the morning light.

4. Always leave a night-light on somewhere in the house, and change its location from night to night. A thief will think that there is someone still awake in the house.

5. If you live in a suburban area and have large grounds or extensive shrubbery, the use of spotlights or floodlights should be considered. They should be positioned so that they do not blind you as you look out and do not annoy the neighbors, but an intruder will know he can easily be seen.

6. Keep the doorway to your home clear of heavy shrubbery. Shrubs may look nice but can afford protection to a lurking intruder who is hiding and waiting your return home.

7. Keep high shrubbery away from all windows also. They can provide excellent cover for a burglar.

8. If you have a garage with a separate door leading into your home, make sure you keep your garage door locked at all times. Once a burglar gets into a garage, he can close the door and then at his leisure work on the house entrance, even using tools and equipment he finds in the garage.

Six Survival Tactics When You Find an Intruder in Your Home

1. If you have gone to bed and awaken and hear an intruder in your house or trying to break in, call the police and make sure you stay calm enough to give them your name and address before you hang up. (Crime experts say a phone should always be kept next to the bed.) After you call, do nothing but wait as quietly as possible for help to arrive.

2. If there is no phone in the bedroom, do not try to get to it, but lock your bedroom door, climb out the window, and try to get to a neighbor or a telephone.

3. If it is impossible to leave through a window, secure the bedroom door, double-locking it with a chair hooked onto the doorknob, and open the window and scream as loud as you can.

4. If your home is too isolated for yelling to be effective, secure the bedroom door and remain perfectly still. Usually, if a burglar finds a locked door, he will reason there is someone in the room and will move away to avoid a confrontation.

5. If you awake and find someone in your bedroom, remain as still as possible. A person in bed is quite defenseless against a prowler and should, if at all possible, avoid an encounter.

6. If worse comes to worst and you come face to face with an intruder, don't panic. Be ready to defend yourself but otherwise stand perfectly still. Don't try to scream and don't try to talk to him. The average burglar is interested only in robbery but will strike out viciously if he feels threatened. If you remain still, he may have time to reason and slowly retreat.

Ten Ways to Burglarproof Your Home While You Are on Vacation

1. Notify your local police department of your absence so that the patrol car covering your area can make periodic checkups.

2. Arrange to have a neighbor pick up your mail and watch for any strangers around your home.

3. Ask your neighbor to pick up any circulars and samples that accumulate at your door. These are the signs a burglar looks for.

4. Cancel all regular deliveries such as milk and newspapers, but don't leave notes saying when you will return.

5. Don't notify the local society columnist about your intended vacation. Buglars read such tidbits. Instead, wait until you get back. You'll have much more to say and can even supply pictures of your trip.

6. If you have a lawn, arrange for someone to come by to cut the grass and clean up the area. This will give your home a lived-in look.

7. Secure all windows and doors with burglarproof security hardware.

8. Never disconnect your telephone while you're on vacation. A disconnected phone is the perfect tip-off to a burglar.

9. Don't draw all venetian blinds or curtains. Be inconsistent: Leave some closed, especially those facing the sun; leave others only partially drawn.

10. Use several automatic light timers in the house; set them for different hours so that there are lights on most of the night somewhere in the house.

Thirteen Breeds to Consider When Choosing a Watchdog

A dog with a good nose can pick up a scent from a quarter mile away. It will often detect an intruder who is still unseen by its master. It can hear, at a great distance, a window being forced or a doorknob being turned. In short, a dog is just about the best automatic burglar alarm a person can have.

If you have a private home and a fair amount of ground, you can have a large watchdog. If you live in an apartment, fairness and humaneness toward the animal require that the dog be of the smaller variety, one that needs less exercise or can get a great deal of it indoors. Here is a list of dogs, large and small, to be considered for their pluses and minuses.

1. German Shepherd. Probably the best of the big watchdogs, provided the dog has large quarters and gets a good deal of outdoor exercise. Highly intelligent and with a great war record, it is the only breed the U.S. Air Force uses.

2. Airedale. Another fine watchdog if it isn't too closely confined. It is important that this dog, like the German Shepherd, not be mistreated, or it will become too aggressive.

3. Giant or Standard Schnauzer. Everything said about the Airedale applies here. It is important that this dog gets good training and has a good relationship with the family. It is important that the dog knows not to attack all strangers automatically.

4. Doberman Pinscher. Generally this breed can be too aggressive for home guard-duty. Remarkably intelligent, it can make an excellent cop against robbers but is tough to train properly and requires an enormous amount of understanding. The U.S. Marine Corps uses the Doberman because of its aggressive nature. The Marines want a fighter or mankiller war dog whereas the Air Force, more interested in a sentry, opts for the German shepherd.

5. Russian Wolfhound. As intelligent and overly aggressive as the Doberman, the Russian wolfhound may develop the same "fault" as the former—one-man-mindedness. It may focus on one member of the family as the master and obey instructions only from that person. If it chooses the man of the house and if he is away at work much of the time, the wife may have a hard time handling it.

6. Chow. Should be classified with the Doberman and the Russian wolfhound in terms of its ability as a watchdog.

7. Pointer. A wonderful bird-hunting breed and very obedient, which will tend to deaden its aggressive qualities.

8. Setter. Same characteristic as the pointer.

9. Spaniel. Another bird hunter with the same deficiencies as a watchdog as the pointer and setter. Naturally, this is a general statement, and, as with all breeds, there are exceptions to the rule.

10. Medium Mongrel (with Shepherd or Terrior Blood). Some of these mixes make better watchdogs than the fussier purebreds. But you are taking a chance with one and can determine such a dog's watching ability only by trial and error. By that time you may be so attached to the animal that you can't get rid of it—even after your home has been burglarized and you realize that your dog must have greeted the intruder or intruders with tail wagging.

11. Bulldog. Can make a good apartment guard but some are handicapped by a rather squeaky, high-pitched bark.

12. Dachshund. One of the most courageous of the small dogs, it is a hunting hound but, unlike the pointer and setter, doesn't lose its aggressive qualities. The dachshund is not so small a dog as it appears. What gives it the appearance of being small is its very short legs, but when you consider the rest of its body and the size of its mouth and teeth, you see it really is a fairly big dog. Very deep-chested, it has a very loud bark, a virtue in a watchdog in a private house or apartment—if you have understanding neighbors.

13. Terriers. Any medium or even small-size terrier, such as the fox terrier, makes a very good watchdog. Terriers have been favorites with European farmers for centuries. In the home they can make enough of a racket to frighten off almost any burglar. One particular favorite is the Yorkshire terrier. Coal miners in England used the Yorkie to go down into the shaft with them to catch mice and rats. The Yorkie is unusually fearless and will attack anything that upsets it, regardless of size. Of course, some of this "fearlessness" may spring from fear. Anything out of the ordinary will upset a Yorkie. It will bark at a box sitting in the middle of the floor where it does not belong. When it hears any strange noise, anything that indicates an intruder, it will bark and often will not obey the master's orders not to bark. This may be disconcerting at times, but the Yorkie does a capital job as a watchdog. Give this game little critter top marks in the little-dog category and the German shepherd top honors in the big-dog category.

Thirteen Tips for the Woman Alone

A few years ago, a prisoner in the Louisiana State Penitentiary drew up a list of do's and don'ts for the woman alone. It was composed in consultation with forty molesters. The tips, plus additions from several police departments, follow.

1. Don't walk near the building line in a poorly lit area where a pair of strong arms can pull you into a hallway or alley.

2. Stay out near the curb and don't be afraid to scream if you fear attack.

3. Don't try judo on an attacker. It might cause him some trouble, but he will probably retaliate. Most molesters agree they would break a woman's wrist or neck if she tried that kind of resistance.

4. If you have a hatpin and know how to use it, do. Most attackers are fearful of hatpins because the damage can be quite severe and can put them in the hospital. The idea is to strike fast, then run. Few attackers will pursue because they know the woman still has the hatpin and will probably strike again before he can stop her.

5. Don't take shortcuts across vacant lots at night and stay clear of billboards.

6. Women drivers should never pick up hitchhikers, male or female, since it can be a big risk.

7. Don't carry your keys in your purse. If a purse snatcher

grabs it, he may beat you home and loot the place. Or he could be waiting for you with rape on his mind.

8. When moving into an apartment, don't list your first name or use Mrs., Miss, or Ms. J. E. Brown could be a mean longshoreman as far as an intruder is concerned.

9. Use only your initials in the telephone directory. This discourages obscene callers; it may also foil a potential intruder trying to discover if the occupant of a certain apartment is a woman.

10. Always insist that you get a new lock on your door when renting a new apartment. If management must have a copy of the key so that the apartment can be entered in case of emergency, give the suprintendent the key in a sealed, taped envelope. This will encourage the super to be more careful with it than with other keys. A favorite method of apartment thieves is to break into the closet where copies of all keys are kept. For some reason, such storage places usually have poor security protection.

11. In self-service elevators that indicate direction enter only when you are sure it will go in the direction you wish. Prop your foot against the door and push your number and see if the elevator is going up from the lobby or down to the basement or garage. If it is going down, step out and wait. Apartment intruders like to wait in the basement and have the elevator bring the victims to them.

12. In a subway, try to ride in the first car, near the motorman. Molesters tend not to operate in the first car because the motorman often has a radio and can signal ahead if there is trouble in the car.

13. In deserted stations or at bus stops, stand near any uniformed person—police, private guard, serviceman, even sanitation man. Statistics show that men in uniform are more likely to "get involved" than other men. Molesters know this, too.

Five Ways to Foil a Pickpocket

Much can be written about the methods of pickpockets but very little on how to counter them. These men, at least the best of them, can rob you while looking you straight in the eye. Here are some defensive measures you can use.

1. Beware of BEWARE OF PICKPOCKETS signs. Pickpockets hang out around such signs because many marks will invariably touch their wallet. This tells the pickpocket where to look, and often a victim touching his wallet has a large amount of cash.

2. When carrying a large sum of money, don't get involved in events on the street. Be very conscious of the money you are carrying. Pickpockets often work in gangs; if you have been spotted with the money, a "show" may be staged to distract you.

3. If you find yourself being jostled in a crowd, ignore the advice not to fan your pocket for fear you will reveal where you are carrying money. Instead, put your hand right over the pocket, keep it there, and move away as soon as you get a chance. Usually two members of a pickpocket trio will "frame" you in a crowd so that you can't move your arms. Then the third member of the gang, perhaps reading a paper or even smiling and talking to you, will pick you clean. Your only defense is to pull your hands free and cover your money. Don't worry about "embarrassing" an innocent party.

4. Don't feel secure when you have your money tucked in a front jacket pocket. Most men regard this as the safest pocket of all. Actually, a good "dip" will find it rather easy to get at, mainly because the victim has lulled himself with the idea that his wallet is in a good place. A pickpocket will catch him in some crowded conveyance, such as an elevator

or a bus, and proceed to "kiss the sucker." Again, his best prop is a newspaper or several packages. At the right moment he will shove the paper in the victim's face or let the packages slip forward. Either way, the victim is off guard and at that moment his wallet is taken.

5. The best way to foil a pickpocket is to split up your money. Put some in your wallet, some in each of your two side pockets, and some in your shirt pocket. If you do that routine in a bank, the spotter for a pickpocket gang will tend to let you go. It will be difficult to clean out all your pockets at once, and you obviously are an alert man. It makes more sense for him to concentrate on the next person, who is putting all his money in one convenient pocket.

IX.
IMPERFECT MURDERS: CRIMES THAT DIDN'T PAY

The Slightly Imperfect Murder #1: Seeds of Guilt

Terry Almodovar decided his wife, Louisa, had to go. The day before the big dance at the Rumba Palace, a wealthy widow had come to his room bearing a number of gifts—a sharp new green suit, some flashy two-tone shoes, and several ties.

"What a pity you're married," said the widow, sighing and pinching Terry's cheek.

Too bad indeed, Terry thought. He was, and had been for some time, a gigolo. But recently he'd made a sad mistake; he'd let himself be guided by his heart instead of his wallet. That was how he happened to marry Louisa. Then Louisa began talking about Terry's getting a regular job and supporting her properly. Terry left Louisa after a mere five weeks of wedded bliss.

Now, thought Terry, if it weren't for Louisa, he could really get the widow to open her purse for him. The next afternoon, Terry called Louisa and told her to meet him at nine P.M. in New York's Central Park. He hinted at a reconciliation but told her not to mention anything about their rendezvous to her family.

The police were called when Louisa's body was found in the early morning of November 2, 1942, in a ditch in the park. She had been strangled. One of two things had happened, the police were sure. Either the slaying was the work of a park marauder, or the killer had to be Terry. Terry played it cool and said nothing.

The police were able to pinpoint the time of death as between nine and ten o'clock the night before. Terry calmly informed them he was wowing the ladies at the Rumba Palace at the time. He knew he would need no faked alibi. And he was right, for the girls flocked to his aid. No fewer than twenty-two of them insisted they'd danced with him during that time. His widow friend insisted he hadn't been out of her sight for more than a minute at a time.

Actually, Terry had had enough time to slip away from the dance, murder his wife in the nearby park, and return. Terry figured he had pulled things off in his usual smooth pattern—and was more than shocked when he was arrested. When he came up for trial he was still shouting denials, insisting he hadn't been in Central Park for at least two years.

Then New York City toxicologist Alexander Gettler took the stand and testified that sand found in Terry's cuffs was the same as that at the murder scene. He'd compared the sand under a spectrograph. Even a few yards from the corpse, the composition of the earth was different. And Terry's new green suit had yielded even more incriminating evidence. It also bore seeds from the *dicot milleflorium* plant, extremely rare in the New York area. It grew in only three spots in Central Park, three localities in Westchester, and two on Long Island. But Professor Joseph Copeland, head of the Botany Department at the College of the City of New York, noted that in only one of these areas was the grass shorter than the normal for *dicot milleflorium*, about one-fiftieth of an inch. That was at the murder scene. And that produced the stunted seed found in Terry's cuffs.

Terry claimed he had gone no further than Broadway and the Rumba Palace—but he had. He had gone to Central Park—to build the perfect case against himself. It took the jury only three minutes to find Terry guilty; he was sent to the electric chair.

The Slightly Imperfect Murder #2: The Upside-Down Affair

No one could accuse Claude and George Oliver of being piggish. They had deliberately let the insurance lapse on Claude's car so insurance fraud wouldn't be suspected. After all, 95 percent of a loaf was better than none.

Claude, thirty-one, and his nephew, George, twenty, were inseperable pals, and that didn't change at all when Claude suddenly married Delia Ringer—she was just added on and they became a trio. People in Davis, Oklahoma, got used to seeing the three of them—always the three of them—driving around together in Claude's broken-down jalopy. Drove mighty fast, too. They sure ought to be more careful, people would say.

That was exactly what the boys wanted people to remember.

Claude and George thought of Delia as nothing but a dollar sign. That was why Claude had convinced his bride that the nicest thing she could do was take out an insurance policy for $5,000—one with a double-indemnity clause in case she died in an accident—with him as beneficiary.

One day, the trio drove to the bridge just outside of town. Delia never had a chance. George beat her over the head with a tire iron and Claude bashed her face in with a rock; the blood spewed down the seat and car floor.

Then the murderous pair moved the car to the bridge rail and pressed the starter, sending the car over the side. It landed upside down in the jagged gully below.

The story the boys told the police was simple: They should have checked the steering mechanism. They knew it was faulty. They'd been going fast, downhill and on a curve, when the steering gear gave way. George had been driving, with his uncle on the outside of the front seat and Delia in the middle. Claude and George had leaped to safety but Delia had been trapped. That's all there was to it, the boys said. They even produced a local cotton picker (bribed with $50) who claimed he'd witnessed the accident.

George and Claude no doubt had begun counting their insurance loot. Unfortunately for them, there was little to do with money on death row at Oklahoma State Prison, which was where they wound up.

The boys hadn't planned their accident well enough. Though Delia's face and skull were battered, there were no bruises on her arms, and a person plunging off a bridge in a speeding car generally throws the hands up to shield the face.

That fact was merely suspicious, however. What really convinced the jury was the location of the victim's blood. Blood had stained the car seat and the floor, but the car had landed upside down, and Delia was lying on her back on the car's ceiling. But there was virtually no blood on the ceiling, where it all should have been. George and Claude were executed on August 23, 1933.

The Slightly Imperfect Murder #3: The Impossible Dream House

Whatever Willie Guldensuppe wanted, Willie Guldensuppe got. He was a big bruiser, used to having his own way, and not averse to using force if necessary. Willie wanted Augusta Nack. He wanted her from the day he moved into the Nack home as a boarder, and he soon began having his own way to such an extent that Mr. Nack moved out of his own house in disgust.

That suited Willie just fine. It was also all right with Augusta, whose head was easily turned. Sadly, Willie did not turn her head for long. There was another boarder, Martin

Thorne, who attracted Augusta. Willie Guldensuppe handled that rivalry in typical fashion. He gave Thorne a beating and booted him out of the house.

One day, Willie returned from work and found Augusta and Thorne alone together. He beat up Thorne again and kicked him out a second time.

Brute force, however, has only limited effectiveness. Augusta really wanted Thorne, and secretly she and Thorne began plotting ways to make their meetings safer. They finally decided their only recourse was to get rid of Willie. And Willie played right into their hands. In an effort to win back Augusta's affections, Willie told her one day that he'd built a little summer cottage—a dainty dream house—just for her.

"It's not all finished," he said, "but let's go out and look it over this weekend. I think it'll make you change your mind about me."

Augusta thought it over. So did Martin Thorne. Augusta told Willie she'd be happy to go with him.

When Willie and Augusta arrived at the partly furnished cottage, the first thing Willie did was step up to the closet to hang up their jackets. He opened the door and was shot dead. Martin Thorne had been inside the closet with a revolver. He also had a butcher knife, a bottle of carbolic acid, and a rope for hanging, just in case. They weren't needed. Willie was dead.

Thorne and Augusta lugged the corpse to the bathtub. At last, they were free of Willie. Now, with plenty of leisure and all the privacy they needed, all they had to do was cut up the body and get rid of it piece by piece and no one would ever know what had become of Willie Guldensuppe.

When the first piece of him was fished out of the East River on June 28, 1897, there was only a torso and no possible way to identify the victim. Thorne and Augusta figured they were safe as long as no identification of Willie's dismembered corpse could lead back to them.

Their plan seemed flawless, and it might have been except for a farmer who wondered why his ducks were turning red. He couldn't figure it out until he found them swimming in a nearby pond that had crimson scum on top. It was the pond right near which a New Yorker had recently put up a cottage.

The farmer called the law, and the trail from the pond led to Augusta and Thorne, for the bloodstains in the cottage indicated foul play and the owner of the cottage had been identified as Willie Guldensuppe.

Willie had told Augusta that his dream cottage was not entirely finished; it was the plumbing that was incomplete. The water lines were in but the sewer pipes were not, and the bathtub merely drained into the pond. As the fiendish killers cut up their victim his blood had drained into the pond. That was the dead giveaway that eventually sent Thorne to the chair and landed his mistress a long prison term.

The Slightly Imperfect Murder #4: Leftovers

The disappearance of Louisa Luetgert was not much of a mystery to the Chicago police. They concluded that Louisa had been murdered by her ever-loving—of other women, that is—husband, Adolph.

Adolph owned the A. L. Luetgert Sausage Works on the North Side, and the police theory was that the missing Mrs. Luetgert had been cooked down to something as easily disposed of as sausage meat itself. Luetgert first came to the attention of the police when he went down to the station house to complain that his wife had a secret lover. The officers were not ready to believe that one; Mrs. Luetgert was a frail, sickly woman, who wouldn't excite many men, and the police also knew that Luetgert himself was quite a cutup with the ladies and often entertained them in his plant after hours.

So the officers did nothing about Luetgert's odd complaint—until sometime later, when Mrs. Luetgert vanished and failed to appear for more than a week. Luetgert's story was that his wife had deserted him for another man. Since Mrs. Luetgert had been seen by friends a half hour before her husband declared they had quarreled and she had left him, the police began nosing around the sausage plant.

A strange odor emanated from one of the vats, and it was drained. But nothing was found except a few unidentifiable bones and a gold wedding ring. Luetgert took one look at the ring and admitted it was Louisa's, but he insisted he had been carrying it around in his vest pocket ever since the bustup—in memory of their happier days. The ring must have dropped from his pocket into the vat while he was working over it, he insisted.

The police found other incriminating evidence; for example, Luetgert had made a large purchase of potash. Potash, when boiled with water, can do a thorough job on the human body. Luetgert's explanation: He was working on a secret formula to develop a new soap. There was no doubt about it—soap with a potash base would certainly remove dirt, all right. The trouble was that it would remove skin, too.

All in all, Luetgert told a mighty shaky tale, and the police had their suspicions, but they could do nothing about them unless they could prove beyond a doubt that Louisa's body had been cooked into sausage meat and disposed of.

So, for a little while, Luetgert went around smirking like a fatted calf—until he was placed under arrest.

The authorities saved their little surprise for Luetgert until the trial: A host of witnesses testified that in recent years Louisa Luetgert's knuckles were so painfully swollen from arthritis that she was unable to remove her wedding ring.

"The only way it could have been gotten off would be for her finger to have melted out of it," Mrs. Luetgert's doctor testified.

And that is precisely what had happened. Adolph Luetgert missed melting in the electric chair. He got life in Joliet.

The Slightly Imperfect Murder #5: The Plot Was All Wet

Since there would be nothing left of the body to indicate foul play, there was no reason for Frederick Small to restrain himself when slaying his wife, Florence. So he beat her over the head with a lead pipe, strangled her with a rope, and, for good measure, shot her.

Then he laughed. When he was through with his clever plan, no one would suspect anything. His wife was going to "burn to death" in a fire that would occur later that day, when Small would be in Boston, miles away from the couple's summer cottage in Mountain View, New Hampshire, on Lake Ossipee.

First, Small got busy with rosin, a cloth, and thermite. Thermite is a substance used in blast furnaces to produce very high heat quickly. Carefully he applied the preparation to the neck, face, and head of his wife. Then he set up a device he had constructed with an alarm clock, batteries, and spark plugs.

Placing the body in the middle of the living room, he doused the room with kerosene and set his timer to produce a spark that would set off the kerosene, rosin, and thermite. The blaze would melt or burn everything—corpse, cottage, bullet, and the infernal machine itself. There would be no clues and the fire would not even start until several hours after Small's departure for Boston. Who could possibly suspect him of murder?

When the taxi arrived a short time later, Small hesitated as he left the cabin and called back inside, "Good-bye, dear. I'm on my way." He seemed to listen to something his wife said and called out again, "No, dear, I won't forget."

At the station Small met a family friend who he knew would be going to Boston also. Once in Boston, Small concentrated on nothing else but making sure he was seen by people who knew him well and could buttress his alibi.

Later that evening, Small caught a train back to his New Hampshire home. Gloating inwardly, he knew all he had to do was feign shock and play the role of the heartbroken husband for a short period, then he could console himself with his wife's fortune.

It was quite a jolt therefore when, on his arrival in Mountain View, Small was immediately arrested for murder. His invention had gone off like clockwork but, as the prosecutor explained later at the trial, "Mother Nature herself had foiled the perfect murder plot."

The fire had broken out, as planned, and had razed the cottage, but the floor had collapsed, and corpse, timer, and all had fallen into the basement, where, unknown to Small, several inches of water had seeped in because heavy rains had raised the level of the lake. The water doused the flames, leaving intact not only the body but also Small's telltale contraption.

That little damper on Frederick Small's perfect murder plot sent him to his execution on January 15, 1918.

The Slightly Imperfect Murder #6: Losing One's Head

The facts about the murder of Madame Gillet, a Parisian milk woman, came out, in a manner of speaking, in bits and pieces. First the police were notified about a human arm and leg that had been found in a hotel closet. The next day, the other leg turned up in a trash basket in Paris' Latin Quarter. The fourth limb was discovered a short time later in a park. A small pond yielded up the torso.

Now all that was still missing was the head, but that was enough to delay identification of Madame Gillet for some time. It was finally made through a scar on her right forearm.

Thus a search was launched for the victim's head and for her killer. One clue the police had was that the killer was a rank amateur at dissection. The dismemberment was a horrible botch, and, according to an examining physician, the killer had apparently done it with a blunt scraper, pounding through the bone joints with a hammer.

The investigation was not going too well. In the first place, there were two killers, not one. Second, they were not amateurs at dismembering bodies. Maurice Barre was a butcher's apprentice, and Pierre Lebiez was a former medical student. They had deliberately cut up the body with unlikely tools and used sloppy techniques just to throw the police off the scent.

The strategy had worked, just as had the choice of

Madame Gillet as a victim. No one would ever suspect that she had been killed for her money because no one knew she'd had any. Maurice Barre was the only one she'd told that she had a number of negotiable securities.

Since the police had gone off the trail because of false clues, it was just as fitting that they should get back on the right track in the same way. A few days after the murder, on an April day in Paris in 1878, a tavern keeper in the Quarter had been robbed and left dying. A huge manhunt was launched to find the killer. During the next week and a half everyone who might conceivably be a suspect was checked out.

Soon attention centered on Maurice Barre, for Barre, police learned, had been on the verge of bankruptcy until about the time of the robbery, when he had suddenly become a lavish spender, seemingly with money to burn. Among Barre's purchases had been a portmanteau, which was laboriously traced to a baggage room in Mans.

When police opened it, they found among a jumble of rags the head of Madame Gillet.

It is very difficult to come up with a good story when you are caught with the victim's head in your possession, and Barre could do nothing but confess. He named Pierre Lebiez as his accomplice.

The killers' downfall had been caused by the most incredible display of bungling in the annals of crime. Each had busied himself after the murder disposing of various parts of the body and the loot in different hiding places. When the portmanteau had been checked at the station, each of the forgetful killers had assumed the other had already disposed of the head!

Because the pair had failed to lose Madame Gillet's head, both lost theirs on the guillotine.

The Slightly Imperfect Murder #7: Sermon of Death

It might be disputed whether or not George Morton Field was the richest man in the small rural community of Mustoch, Kansas. There was no argument that he was the most stiff-necked. A man of God, with a stern religious code, he contributed much of the money that built the local church. And when no itinerant preacher was available, Field himself would take to the pulpit to make the sinners in the congregation squirm like abandoned souls.

One person in the congregation, however, failed to heed Field's fire-and-brimstone sermons—Field himself. He fell victim to the weakness of human flesh in the ample form of one Gertie Day, a rollicking, rosy-cheeked girl who had a way with men. Gertie sang in the choir and the trouble began when Field asked her to remain after choir practice. Before he knew it, Field was threatened with a scandal. When Gertie found she was pregnant, she became hysterical. Field would have to do right by her, she said. She would have her baby and keep quiet about the father—provided Field paid her for the child's upkeep. That would have been reasonable to Field except that he pictured himself living in constant fear that someday Gertie would reveal his secret.

Field came up with the only sound solution. Both Gertie and her unborn child would be better off in some other world, and Field went about plotting how to transport them there. He went to Kansas City to buy dynamite and other necessary ingredients for making a bomb.

Field had no problem getting Gertie to the church late one night. He had promised to have $2,000 for her. Gertie arrived on time, and while she awaited for the arrival of her salvation Field was under the church, ready with his bomb. He had been most careful preparing his instrument of death, even wrapping it in paper so that his fingerprints would not be found on any part of the bomb after the blast. Field lit a ten-minute fuse and raced back home. He was there when the explosion roused the entire community. With all his neighbors, Field rushed to the demolished church. It was morning before enough of Gertie was found to be identifiable. She was known to have had plenty of admirers and almost anyone could have had a rendezvous with her at the church. And almost anyone could have blown up the church to kill her.

Sheriff James R. Carter poked around in the ruins and found bits of the bomb, then drove back to his office in Atchison. Field was not even questioned. He was, he was sure, quite safe.

But he wasn't. Sheriff Carter already knew that the erstwhile man of God was the murderer. With Field's picture, Carter spent the next five days checking out stores in Kansas City. A hardware clerk recognized Field as the man who had bought wires from him just before the date of the explosion.

When the sheriff called on Field, he passed along this troubling information, then handed him a charred piece of paper. Field gazed at his own handwriting. In his effort to be careful he had wrapped the bomb in paper and unwittingly had used a copy of one of his sermons. It is a quirk of dynamite that often elements nearest the explosion escape with much less damage than matter farther away. The words on the paper were quite clear: "The wrath of God will slay all sinners."

Sinner Field was sentenced to life in the state penitentiary and died there eleven years later, in 1926.

The Slightly Imperfect Murder #8: Garden of Evil

Mrs. Catherine Tinker, an English widow, was a prime candidate for murder. Living in the south of France, in a large villa outside Marseilles, she hired no servants and mixed very little with neighbors. About the only ones she made friends with were André and Marthe Dentu, who lived in an adjoining villa. Unfortunately, the Dentus were criminals who merely used the villa as a retreat from their underworld activities whenever things got too hot. That they bothered to strike up an acquaintance with Mrs. Tinker at all was a case of mixing business with pleasure. They realized the old woman was a natural target for robbery. She had many jewels and a houseful of other valuables. If their neighbor disappeared, the Dentus reasoned, no one would notice or care much if they did notice.

Madame Dentu did the actual killing. Slipping up behind the old woman as she sat on her veranda, Marthe strangled her with a length of wire. Then the Dentus hurriedly dragged the body into their own house before any prying eyes could observe them. Once the corpse was safely indoors, they began a systematic looting of Mrs. Tinker's home. They carried off her poorly hidden caches of cash and jewels and, after dark, moved the bulkier items, such as priceless antiques, into their house. The following day, the household goods were shipped by van to a fence in Marseilles.

With the loot stashed away, the Dentus then could concentrate on the problem of what to do with Mrs. Tinker's body. They dumped it in their bathtub and then purchased several big carboys of concentrated sulfuric acid. Working carefully, they filled the tub with acid until the body was covered. The corpse dissolved very slowly, so each day the Dentus had to lug containers of the diluted acid to their yard and dump them there in holes they had dug for the job. It took two weeks for the task to be completed, but at last the Dentus relaxed. They had their loot and their victim had disintegrated into shapeless blobs, which they'd conveniently buried.

True, the killers realized, Mrs. Tinker would eventually be missed, but what of it? There would be no reason for the police to be any more suspicious of the Dentus than of the victim's other neighbors.

A few days later, the Dentus returned to their criminal haunts in Marseilles. They planned that on their return to their villa, and if anyone asked, they would simply say they knew nothing about when or why Mrs. Tinker vanished.

Imagine their chagrin upon their return when they found themselves immediately placed under arrest. The police had dug up their yard while they were away and retrieved several bits of human flesh and bone. Stunned, the Dentus broke down and confessed to the murder, asking only that the police explain why they had been suspected.

The acid they had dumped in their yard, obliging officers said, gradually had poisoned the entire garden. The grass and plants in a wide circle around the burial place had died off until, finally, only a huge black spot remained. As the acid's poison spread, the garden of a neighbor was similarly affected. He had complained to the authorities, and suspicious police had dug up the Dentus' garden. They had found the grisly remains of a body and concluded they were parts of the missing widow.

The Slightly Imperfect Murder #9: Spur of the Moment

They draped the body carefully over the tracks, laying the head neatly on one rail and the legs across the other rail. Leone Gagliardi and Angelo Donofrio nodded to each other with satisfaction. After the train passed over him, the body would be so cut up that no one would ever suspect he had been beaten to death before the train ever touched him.

The pair returned to Montreal and Gagliardi went to see his sweetheart, Tomasina Sarao, who happened to be the victim's wife. But now she was a widow, a young widow. And since her husband, Nicolas, had taken out a large insurance policy, she would be a rich widow. Tomasina and Gagliardi were going to live happily ever after.

It was not until the following day that Antonio Sarao went to Montreal police headquarters to report his father missing. The police had already found the victim's body. The police wanted to know if the father had any reason for going out near the Blue Bonnets racetrack.

Young Sarao nodded. "Yes, someone had mentioned seeing an ad in the paper for a gardener and my father went to see about the job." The police were interested in who had told him about the job. The youth thought a moment. "It was my stepmother. She said Leone Gagliardi had stopped by to tell her about the advertisement."

The police picked up Leone Gagliardi. First they wanted Gagliardi to produce the ad about the job. He said he couldn't remember where he had seen it.

"It isn't important," said Assistant Inspector Armand Brodeur. "All that matters is that you sent him to that area and he ended up murdered. It was a well-thought-out murder plan and you had to be the key."

Gagliardi shook his head. "No, it was an accident. He was hit by a train. You can't prove he wasn't killed by a train."

Inspector Brodeur laughed. "I can prove that a lot easier than you can prove that he was. The railroad track you laid the body on is a spur to the racetrack and is used only during the racing season. There hasn't been a train over those tracks in months."

On March 29, 1935, Gagliardi, Donofrio, and Tomasina were hanged.

The Slightly Imperfect Murder #10: Branded

The body of William Kappen, a St. Louis electrician, was found in July 1937 in a clump of bushes near the Mississippi River, in Illinois. There was one interesting fact that the police kept secret. They hoped it would lead them to his murderer.

On the day Kappen's body was discovered, he had been due in church to be married. He hadn't shown up. Friends found his wedding clothes laid out on his bed. When he was found dead, it was obvious he had been kidnapped and killed.

The police investigation followed two lines of thought. Either Kappen had been killed because of his involvement with some other woman who resented his upcoming marriage, or else he had been killed by someone who stood to gain financially from his death. The first theory didn't look promising. Kappen and his fiancée had gone steady for three years, and it had been the first romantic involvement for each. But Kappen did have a sister, Marie Porter, who stood to profit from a $3,300 life-insurance policy if her brother died. Furthermore, it was known that Kappen had been planning to make his wife the beneficiary after the marriage.

But Marie Porter, the obvious suspect, had an airtight alibi. During the time Kappen had been killed, she had been entertaining a number of friends. Besides, the lady didn't have the telltale signs the police were looking for. But as officers were leaving Marie Porter's house, after questioning her, they heard her call out to a young daughter that she was going to the drug store for some skin salve and some sleeping pills . . . because the ordeal of the tragedy had been too much for her. Perhaps, after all, she did have the telltale signs. A tail was put on her.

An hour later, police followed the woman to another house. They went in after she left and questioned Angelo Giancola. Yes, he admitted, the Porter woman had brought him the salve. He had a poison-ivy rash on both arms. Giancola, Marie Porter's lover, had a ready alibi for the rash. He explained that he must have picked it up the previous day playing ball at a picnic. A friend of his had picked up the same rash. Although the friend did have a rash, the police weren't satisfied that Giancola had gotten his the same way.

Their doubts were justified. A search of the house eventually produced the murder gun and a confession from Giancola. He had killed Kappen at Marie Porter's instigation. The murderous lovers both went to the chair.

Angelo Giancola would never have come under suspicion had not his beloved bought him the skin salve. The police had been on the lookout for that. William Kappen's body had been found in the middle of a huge patch of the telltale poison ivy.

The Slightly Imperfect Murder #11: Blood Will Tell

Elijah Thompson, Jr., had for weeks watched Helen Jean Bryant, a sixteen-year-old high-school girl from Aliquippa, Pennsylvania, trudge down the wooded hill each morning to the street below for the school bus. But usually she was with other girls. On the morning of October 25, 1954, Helen Jean had come down alone—to be raped and killed by Elijah Thompson.

Only after it was all over did Thompson notice for the first time that there was blood on his trousers, Helen Jean's blood. It put the indelible brand of murderer on him. For a moment Thompson was struck with terror. Then, suddenly, he remembered. Helen Jean had Type-O blood. It was, of course, odd that he should know that, since never in his life had he spoken to the girl. But once, as he had hidden in the bushes near the path the girls took down the hill, he had heard Helen Jean say that she had Type-O blood.

Thompson had the same blood type. He remembered feeling a certain kinship with the girl because of this fact. Now he saw a way out of his dilemma. Later that same evening, he drove to nearby Rochester, Pennsylvania, and got into a fight with a man. He was dripping blood when, after being slammed through a window during the fight, he was rushed to a nearby hospital.

When Helen Jean's body was found, the police came to question Thompson. He knew they would, since he was a neighbor and had a record that included a dishonorable discharge from the army and a stay in prison. The police thought they had something when they found his bloodied clothes, but Thompson had a good story ready, one that the authorities in Rochester would back up. Thompson wasn't worried when the police took a blood sample and his bloodstained trousers with them. He knew that would get them nowhere.

Thompson's dream world did not last long. The next day, the police came to arrest him for the murder of Helen Jean Bryant. Thompson, stunned, kept insisting that it was his blood on his clothes. But the police now knew that not all of it was.

True, both the girl and Thompson had the same blood type. But the police found out a little more about his blood. He had recently picked up a case of venereal disease, and that had showed up in some of the blood from his clothing—but not in all of it. Some of the blood stains did not indicate disease, as Helen Jean's blood did not. Elijah Thompson, Jr., died in the chair, having learned the crimelab axiom that blood will tell.

The Slightly Imperfect Murder #12: The Sit-Down Corpse

There was bad blood between British Army Sergeant Emmett Dunne and Sergeant Tich Watters in Duisburg, Germany. Dunne wanted Watters' wife for himself, and in 1953 he did something about it: He slammed the edge of his hand into Watters' Adam's apple. Watters died instantly and, of course, without bloodshed. The murderous attack had taken place in Dunne's car after Dunne lured Watters away from their barracks to go for a ride.

Then Dunne put Watters' body on the floor in the back of the car and covered it with a blanket. Thirty minutes later, he drove back to the camp and strung up a noose in an empty barracks. A few hours later, Watters' body was found hanging there. It seemed an open-and-shut case of suicide.

Authorities marked the case closed. It remained closed for

fifteen months, during which time Dunne returned to Britain and married Watters' widow. When an old army buddy from Duisburg happened to meet them, it made him think about Watters' death. A report went to higher-ups and they started thinking, too. It was possible that Watters' death had been too readily judged a suicide. A full-scale investigation was launched.

Watters' grave was opened and a careful autopsy made. Doctors found there was no way of telling from the neck injuries if they had been caused by hanging or something else. But blood again told the tale. If Watters had killed himself, he would have been the most remarkable suicide in history—the only person ever to have hanged himself in a sitting position. There was no accumulation of blood in the lower parts of the corpse, which is always the case if a person is hanged. The blood will flow to the feet. But in Watters' case it hadn't. Pathologists were able to determine that Watters had been in a crumpled-up position for more than a half hour after he died. Faced with this evidence, Dunne confessed and went to prison.

The Slightly Imperfect Murder #13: Clues, Clues, Clues

Without doubt the most inept murderer in American history was Robert Latimer, who decided to kill his sixty-year-old widowed mother in 1889 to collect her insurance. Latimer and his mother lived in Jackson, Michigan, and the son went to Detroit to establish an alibi the day before the planned murder. Everything he did after that was wrong. On the night of the murder he was seen slipping out of his Detroit hotel right after registering, and later he was seen slipping back in the early-morning hours. In addition, the maid noticed that his bed had not been slept in.

The bungling Latimer was also seen on the train to Ypsilanti, where he switched trains to catch one bound for Jackson. This brilliant maneuver resulted in his being remembered not by one but by two conductors. Furthermore, on the train back to Detroit, Latimer got into a row with a conductor when he discovered he could not obtain a sleeping berth. In addition, a Detroit barber remembered seeing blood on his shirt on the morning after the murder. Latimer couldn't have done more to sentence himself to life imprisonment if he had carried a sign proclaiming his guilt.

BRICKS, CONS
AND GYPS

X.
TRICKS, CONS, AND GYPS

Nine Con Games

1. Big Spender. Count Victor Lustig, the con man who made the money-making machine famous, believed in flimflamming everyone as a matter of principle. He originated one of the con men's favorite tricks, that of "tishing a lady." Lustig was highly addicted to brothels and always paid well—after a fashion. Upon bidding a lady farewell, he would flash a fifty-dollar bill, fold it up, lift up her dress, and make a play of tucking it in her stocking while actually palming it in a switch. The count would warn her it was trick money and, should she take it out before morning, it would turn to tissue paper. She removed the money as soon as the count left and it had indeed turned to tissue paper.

2. Sweet Racket. John W. Gates was the champion gambler of all time. Once he tried to place a single million-dollar bet on a horse and the bookmakers ran for cover, from that time on referring to him as Bet-a-Million Gates. Gates, however, was not as wild a bettor as was generally believed. One of his favorite bets was the fly game. He was sitting one day at a restaurant table with wealthy playboy John Drake, whose father was a former governor of Iowa and the founder of Drake University. Gates dunked a piece of bread in his coffee and put it on a saucer. "You do the same," he said, "and whoever attracts the most flies to his piece of bread wins. How about a thousand dollars a fly?" Drake took him up on it and promptly lost $11,000. Thereafter Gates worked the trick regularly and always won at it. None of his opponents ever figured out that he was fixing the flies. They also never noticed that he never finished his cup of coffee. Who would, with six spoons of sugar in it?

3. Ten Thousand Hangovers. In all the history of crimping, no man ever kidnapped more sailors than did Shanghai Kelly. During the 1870s, in San Francisco, Kelly provided no fewer than 10,000 unwilling seamen for sailing vessels. Once, Kelly had to turn up ninety men for three ships on the same night. He promptly organized a "sex excursion," renting for it an old steamboat that he loaded with a couple dozen whores and several bartenders. The suckers were promised three days of fun with all the wine and women they could handle. When he had the required ninety head aboard, Kelly cast off and opened barrels of doped liquor. The men woke up the next day in the middle of the blue Pacific, and Kelly collected twice, from the sex-excursion tickets he'd sold and for his shanghai work.

4. The Best Fake in Town. The famed Cardiff Giant hoax was perpetrated by George Hull of Cardiff, a village near Syracuse, New York. Obtaining a five-ton block of gypsum, Hull commissioned a sculptor to make him a naked giant and then pretended that he'd found it on his land. The giant became an overnight sensation as the fossil of a prehistoric man. Hull made considerable money displaying it and even turned down an offer of a princely sum from P. T. Barnum for it. Undaunted, Barnum went ahead and had one of his own giants made and exhibited it as the Cardiff Giant. He took in far more money with his fake than Hull did. Even after Hull's hoax was exposed, Barnum kept making money, displaying his giant as the "authentic fake."

5. The Hard Way. During the Alaska gold rush the town of Skagway was filled with men with ready money—miners who'd struck it rich and a steady flow of hopeful new prospectors. But the man who made the most out of the Klondike strike was Soapy Smith, a gambler who clipped them coming and going. He robbed suckers in his saloon and gambling joint, and had other dodges for picking up loose change. Soapy ran a telegraph office and charged five dollars for sending a wire anywhere. Scores of men sent out telegrams daily and within a matter of hours everyone would get back a five-dollar collect wire in response. It was all quite remarkable, since Skagway had no telegraph line.

6. Ash Magic. During the 1920s a shrewd swindler in Munich named Franz Tausend soaked backers out of more than $100,000 by convincing them he'd found a chemical formula for making gold from lead. He proved it in a number of experiments in which all the necessary equipment and materials were supplied by the suckers themselves so there was no apparent chance of fakery. His victims were so awed that they advanced him money to go into full-scale production. Naturally, he never did. Tausend's trick was not discovered until 1929. He performed his miracle in his secret way and within two hours produced a tiny piece of gold. During that time one of his assistants would hand him a cigarette containing gold dust. Finally, a watcher spotted Tausend flicking the ashes into the compound.

7. Master Touch. The Jimmy Valentine who can open any safe with a few flicks of the tumblers is a figure of fiction. But the greatest safecracker of all time, Herbert Emerson Wilson, who stole $16 million, once convinced members of his own gang that he could perform such a feat. Once, when the gang broke into the offices of a big Chicago business firm, Wilson blithely informed his bewildered confederates that he was forsaking the use of any "soup," drills, or blowtorch. He opened the huge safe, containing thousands of dollars, by manipulation only. The gang was so overawed by Wilson's feat that he didn't have the heart to tell them that he'd noticed the combination of the safe crayoned on the metal top.

8. Legal Loophole. Judge Roy Bean was perhaps the sorriest jurist who ever tried a case in the Old West. He never judged a case on its merits if he knew the party involved. Once a railroader friend of his killed a Chinese laundryman in an argument over some wash. Bean quickly leafed through a dog-eared copy of the *Revised Statutes of Texas* of 1879, which was his sole legal text, and then tossed it aside and announced his verdict: "I don't find nothing in the statutes of the state of Texas that says it's agin the law to kill a Chinaman. Case dismissed."

9. Suckers Beware. Wilson Mizner, the fabled swindler, had the remarkable ability of instantly seeing a way to make a dishonest dollar out of any ordinary happening. Once, Mizner was with a rich son of a Seattle lumber baron and the young man mentioned he had a terrific hangover and couldn't remember what had happened the previous evening. "I'm not surprised," Mizner said. "You were drinking like a fish, but that was some party you threw. I'd say it was the biggest and wildest of the year." Then Mizner hustled over to confer with the maître d'hôtel of a leading Manhattan lobster palace and worked up a phony bill of nearly $2,000 for the imaginary party. The young man paid off, though still befuddled, and Mizner and the maître d'hôtel split the profits.

Once, in Atlantic City, Mizner was walking with a compulsive gambler named Tomlinson when they spotted a man's feet, clad in white buckskin shoes, projecting from a second-floor window of a hotel along the Boardwalk. They got into a dispute of whether or not you could judge a man's height by his shoe size. Since the shoes were at least size eleven, Tomlinson was willing to bet a thousand dollars that the man had to be over five feet nine. Mizner said he'd be less. The bet was made and the men hurried up to the hotel room and found the man with the size elevens sticking out the window. He was a midget who said he just happened to like roomy shoes. Tomlinson paid off and didn't learn for many years that Mizner had planted the midget in the window.

Eight Carnival Gyps

At least 100 million people in the United States will visit some kind of carnival, fair, or bazaar this year, and almost all of them will play a game of skill or a game of chance. Almost all will lose. Carnival games never give a person an even break. This was discovered by the producers of television's *60 Minutes* program, which recently devoted a third of an hour to an exposé of a particularly dishonest game, razzle, in which the player never wins. The rest of the games let the player win, but only once in a while. Perhaps you will still want to go to carnivals and try your hand, but it is at least comforting to know why and how you lose.

1. Penny Pitch. There are those who say penny pitch has the best payoff rate at a carnival. Perhaps that's true. One investigator counted 2,000 pennies tossed in at a penny-pitch game at an amusement park. The payout return was 400, a return rate of 20 percent. Of course, this does not mean that the 400 pennies were lost to the game operators. They were for the most part tossed back in and the payout amount would then drop to 80 pennies.

2. Bushel Basket. Step right up and try your skill at putting three baseballs in the basket for a mere quarter. Get all three in and you win a terrific coffee maker, get two in and you get a great toaster, one or none in and you lose. Of course, the baseballs must stay in the basket. That's the hard part, even though the operator keeps demonstrating how easy it is. The reason it won't work for you is that the baskets have solid, wood-reinforced bottoms that make the ball bounce back. The baskets are tipped toward the player at an angle, and the greater the angle, the more likely that the balls will bounce out. This will happen even more often when the ball hits the upper half of the basket bottom, which it does over 90 percent of the time. Meanwhile, the operator keeps popping balls in and they stay. He has an angle, and that angle is the fact that he's on the other side of the counter. He can toss in balls that don't hit the upper half of the bottom of the basket but, rather, hit down low or else hit the sides of the bushel and simply bounce to the other side and remain inside.

3. Milk-Bottle Toss. All right, you know the gimmick here. The bottle is lead-weighted on the bottom so that there is no way even a Tom Seaver can knock it off its pedestal with a direct hit. But then you are befuddled because the game operator steps out in front of the counter and proceeds to pop the bottles right off. So it must be an honest game . . . and snowmen live on the equator. Not all the bottles are lead-weighted, however—only the bottom three. Only the bottom ones can't be knocked off. When the operator wants to demonstrate how easy it is to do, he simply stacks the bottles the other way around, with the three light ones on the bottom and the three heavy ones on the top two rows. Now the bottles will fall like cream puffs.

4. Nail-Hammering Game. This is a game for fleecing the macho type. The object is to hammer a nail into a railroad tie with one blow of the hammer. The game isn't fixed, obviously, because the operator, time and again, does it effectively. He will pull several nails from a carpenter's apron he's wearing and start them into the railroad tie, which is mounted on two wooden horses. Then he bangs them in, one after the other, with one blow on each. Simple. Now pay your money and try it. You try and you botch it. But you keep playing because the operator starts boosting the odds to 2 to 1 and then 3 to 1. He could make it 100 to 1 because you just aren't going to win. The secret's in the nail and the apron. The apron has a secret inside pocket, which contains some extra-hard nails that will go into the wood with one good blow. But the main part of the apron holds soft nails that bend easily. Superman could not drive them into a hard railroad tie with one blow. Of course, since all the nails seem to come out of the same pocket, a player assumes it's all aboveboard. At times, to allay suspicion, the operator will let the player pick the nail he wants out of a bunch in his hand. Of course, they are all soft losers. This game is such a challenge to manhood that some players lose fifty or a hundred dollars.

5. Ring a Peg. Now step right up to a game you can't lose. You pitch till you win. You pay your fifty cents and get as many rings as you need to encircle an upright wooden peg on an elevated three-by-four platform some four feet behind the counter. The platform holds 156 or more pegs, some worth five, ten, or twenty dollars. This is determined by the number at the bottom of the peg. If the law ever checks the setup, there has been no hanky-panky. The big prizes are there. The rest of the prizes are known as "slum"—five-cent ashtrays, whistles, tie clips, and so on. That's what the suckers win. The game is an incredibly easy one to gaff, or fix. The operator has marked the pegs bearing the big prizes—only a handful of them—so he always knows where they are. Then, if one of them is ringed, he moves between the platform and the customer as he removes the ring. As he blocks the player's view he lifts off the ring and removes not that peg but the one next to it. The pegs are so close together that this flimflam is simple to pull.

6. Hoop and Block. This is another hoop-tossing game; the prizes are really big ones, and all you have to do to win is toss a hoop over a prize and encircle the small wooden block it's displayed on. The hitch: There's a metal rod projecting from the center of each block that makes the game far more difficult than it looks. If the hoop is to clear the rod, it must drop straight down from above. But all the hoops the players toss come in at an angle, and even a very well-aimed toss will usually hit the rod. On the other hand, the operator is inside the counter and close enough to drop a hoop over any prize and block without hitting the rod. He makes it look easy—but it's not.

7. Fish Game. Wander over to the fish-pond game, in which about 100 wooden fish float in a stream of water flowing down a narrow channel past the game counter. The player uses a small rod with a line and hook to catch the fish. Each fish has a hidden slide with a number written on it. If it's one of the selected numbers, it wins a really big prize, such as a television set or record player. If it's a loser, you get some slum. Nobody ever seems to get the big winners, which are posted up on the wall: 9, 16, 18, 66, 89, and 98. But in case the authorities come around to check, they are all there for the inspector to see, and they are as easy to fish out as any other number. In fact, they are fished out quite often, but the player still doesn't win. Run through the winning numbers again: 9, 16, 18, 66, 89, 98. Notice anything? Turn them upside down and read them: 6, 91, 81, 99, 68, 86. All those numbers are losers. It all depends on which way the operator holds the slide as he shows you the number.

8. Mouse Game. This is usually the most crowded one on the midway. The mouse is so cute and surely there's no way to fix a mouse. Or is there? A large revolving wheel is divided into sections numbered from 1 to about 60, and there is a small hole in each numbered section. The operator then places a mouse in the center of the horizontal wheel and covers him up with a tin can. The wheel is spun vigorously and then the operator lifts off the tin can and the mouse, dizzy from the spinning, hesitates for a short time, staggers about, and then ducks into one of the sixty numbered holes for safety. If the number of the hole is the one you have bet on, you can cop the big prize. If several people have the same number, they all get paid off. But that mouse seems to have ways of looking out for the operator's financial interests. He hardly ever seems to pick a number with a lot of bets on it. Like most other carnival games, the mouse game produces enormous profits when operated honestly, but a crooked operator can really fix that mouse. There will be a mechanical gadget under the wheel that can close every other hole. The operator will look over the betting counter and if he sees the big money is on an odd number, he'll close the odd numbers. Mr. Dizzy Mouse may head for that number but when he finds his exit blocked, he'll simply head for a hole that's open to him. Naturally, there is no suspicion attached to the fact that a mouse seems to head for a certain number and then suddenly turns away. What do you expect from a dizzy mouse?

Five Shortchanging Rackets

If the average American were asked to name criminal activities, he'd cite pickpocketing, bank robbery, shoplifting, and so on. He probably would not mention shortchanging, which is a $500-million-a-year crime. There are professional shortchangers who work at jobs not so much for the salary but for what they can steal from the customers. In the recent past, cashiers at crooked circuses and carnivals paid as much as a hundred dollars a week—and received no salary—just for the privilege of handling, and mishandling, cash for the public. Police bunco squads estimate that there are 5,000 professional shortchangers operating in the United States today. Here are some of their techniques.

1. The Drop. Used in various business, it is a favorite with crooked bartenders. A man pays for a $1.10 drink with a twenty-dollar bill. The bartender will make sure he hands back a lot of loose silver, putting the coins and the paper money down on the bar after counting it very deliberately in front of the patron. Then, as the customer is picking up the change, the bartender will recount the bills, straightening them carefully by tapping them on the bar and handing them over in a neat stack. The patron has now seen the paper money counted twice and is certain the amount is accurate. Naturally, he tucks it away in his pocket without giving it another thought. Actually, he has been robbed right in front of his eyes. While the customer was picking up the change and watching the bartender stack the bills neatly, what he failed to notice was that when the bartender tapped the bills on their edges, he let the back bill—the one farthest from the customer—slip off and drop behind the bar amid several bottles stacked there in advance. The bartender can retrieve the money later, but if in the meantime the customer notices he's short, the bill can suddenly be found.

2. The Rip. This is a gimmick that started in carnivals where ticket booths were built high—and, incidentally, ticket booths were built high because it made it easier for shortchanging. The rip is a sleight-of-hand gimmick. Like the drop, it depends on the way the change is counted out. It is also done frequently at check-cashing services. A person cashing a check always counts along with the cashier. A crooked cashier will give the customer two counts, both honest, before sticking the money through the window. First the cashier holds the neatly stacked bills in his left hand so they stick out above the thumb and fingers, but as he hands them over he switches the money to his right hand. And right there the customer is robbed. As he changes hands the cashier's left thumb holds back the top bill, which is usually a ten, since most checks cashed at a check-cashing service range from ninety to two hundred dollars. While the right hand is blocking the customer's view of the left hand the cashier's active left thumb crumples the bill into his left palm. Meanwhile, as he shoves out the rest of the money he turns the pile over so that the stack of ones is on top. Only a complete recount will show a ten-dollar shortage, but hardly anyone will recount, since the money has already been counted out twice. The unsuspecting customer usually stuffs the money into a wallet and walks away.

3. The Walkaway. This is a small dodge used by cashiers at movie houses, circuses, sporting contests, carnivals, and any other place where money is handled in a booth. The secret of the technique's success lies in the fact that all booths are built in such a way that there is some small area that the customer can't see. Shortchangers call this the blind spot and mark off its boundaries. Whenever the cashier makes change, he or she leaves a small part of it in the blind spot. The customer often obliges by grabbing the ticket and the visible change, and walks off. But if the customer counts the money and demands the rest, the cashier can coldly point at the missing change and make the ticket buyer cringe in embarrassment.

4. The Double Count. This is done best in stores when a customer makes a small purchase, say for ninety cents, and pays with, say, a ten-dollar bill. The clerk counts the purchase first, saying, "Ninety [purchase] and ten is one dollar; two, three, four, five, six, seven, eight, nine, and ten [another dime] and ninety [the purchase again]. Thank you." This always happens quite fast and sounds so logical that most people don't notice they are paying for the item twice—first and last. If the customer objects, a correction is immediately made. More often, however, if the customer does notice something, it's that he has gotten two dimes. Sometimes he figures there's been a dime error in his favor and he is anxious to get away from the register. Sometimes he thinks the cashier has made an error in the customer's favor and he returns the dime, leaving with the contented feeling that he is an honest man.

5. The Cabby Count. Police experts estimate that a practiced cabby can add more than a hundred dollars a week to his earnings by shortchanging. The cabby count relies solely on hesitation. The driver starts talking like crazy when you hand him a five or a ten to pay for a small fare. He tucks it in a pocket quickly and continues to talk while preparing to make change. He looks at the meter and calls out the amount shown very deliberately. Then he makes a big deal about giving the passenger the coin change and then he hesitates. That's when it can happen. If the passenger is in a hurry or has been sufficiently distracted by the cabby's spiel, there's a fair chance he will depart without thinking of the missing change in bills. If the passenger doesn't move to leave, the driver counts out the bills. The whole delay is only a second or two, and most passengers who do wait for the full amount are unaware of the stall, so the driver is taking no risk. Also, he has an important fact in his favor. He has to fool the passenger for only a moment to get him out of the cab. After the taxi drives off, there's nothing the customer can do if he suddenly remembers that he didn't get the right change. A cab isn't like a store; you can't find it again in the same place.

Six Communications from the C.O.D. Ghouls

"C.O.D." stands for "collect on death." Whenever a person dies, his survivors may find themselves deluged by mail from death ghouls who do nothing but read the obituary pages and try to collect. The files of police bunco squads and Better Business Bureaus bulge with complaints lodged by victims. The approaches resemble the following samples assembled for this book:

1. "Dear Scotty," a letter will begin to the newly deceased. "How are you, old man? Well, I just got back to town today and as I promised, I'm dropping you a line so we can get together soon. Ran into Bob Hamilton in Syracuse the other day and he told me to pass along his regards. . . . Oh, say, old man, I hate to bring it up, but I hope you can return that $75 I loaned you a few months ago at the ——— Lodge. You remember what I was telling you about the missus, about not knowing if it was serious or not. Well, it looks pretty bad now, and I'm pressed with bills, so I hope you can come through for me. But you know, that isn't the only reason I want to get together with you again. As you said, we just don't see enough of each other." Of course, all the fraud has done is taken the dead man's name from the death notices. Most grief-stricken families send a check immediately when they receive such a letter.

2. "Dear Friend," the letter reads, and enclosed is a bill for thirty dollars. "Enclosed please find the beautiful leather-bound Bible with your name [the dead man's] embossed on the cover that you recently ordered. We are sure it will give you many years of joyful and devout contentment." Most grieving widows will pay that bill. After all, this Bible is probably the last thing her husband bought. It comes now as

though it's a message to her from her husband . . . or even from God.

3. "Dear Mrs. ———," a postcard from a clipping agency reads. "A news item relating to your late husband in a publication of large and wide circulation has come to the attention of our New York office. We feel it would be a fitting item to add to the treasury of your loved one's mementos. Upon receipt of five dollars, we shall be happy to supply you with a clipping suitably mounted for lasting beauty." Eager to have this item, the widow quickly sends off the money and gets back the obituary or perhaps only the printed death notice that she paid to have published in the local paper. She has no legal redress. The local paper is a publication of large circulation. And wide circulation as well. Why, an out-of-town newsstand in Times Square sells papers from every part of the country. Wouldn't you call up to 3,000 miles away wide circulation? As for suitable mounting, what can you expect for five bucks other than the clipping scotch-taped to an index card?

4. No written communication here, but, as they say, one picture is worth a thousand words. A large carton is delivered and inside is a striking oil painting of the deceased. The return label says something like *Alfred L. K. Andrews, Portraits*. The following day a bill from Andrews arrives for $2,500. It would appear that the deceased had posed for the portrait sometime before his death. It *is* a lot of money but it is something to remember him by, much better than a mere photograph. Of course, the painting was copied from a recent photograph. One con artist was sent to prison after years of making at least $30,000 annually out of this routine. He got caught when he painted brown eyes on a blue-eyed man.

5. "Dear Madam," this one from some obscure "investment" company begins. "We have been advised of your late husband's recent death and have tried to delay intruding on your bereavement for as long as possible. However, we must assume you have found records among your husband's effects concerning his purchase of certain bonds from our company. He had made an initial payment of $2,500 and unless we receive the balance of the final $2,500, his option must be considered canceled and the original payment forfeit. Please be advised that final payment date is ten days from the above

date." A widow will think twice about losing a $2,500 investment. If she pays, she is getting a bargain—$5,000 of worthless bonds for only $2,500.

6. The same sort of letter as in the preceding case but this one is about land in Florida that the late husband was buying as a surprise for his wife when they retired.

Five Rules for Beating the Death Ghouls

Police bunco squads and the Better Business Bureau offer some simple rules to keep grieving survivors from being victimized.

1. After a death occurs in the family, don't transact any but the most essential business until everyone has fully recovered from the shock.

2. If you are not completely familiar with the details of a transaction, do not deal with strangers.

3. Do not sign any papers. Death ghouls have been known to thrust papers before a grieving widow with an extra digit inserted, raising a charge enormously.

4. Do not accept any COD packages.

5. Always investigate before you pay a bill you know nothing about.

XI.
UNUSUAL WAYS TO AVOID DEATH AND OTHER PUNISHMENTS

Five Ways to Beat the Rap

1. The Legs Diamond Erasure Method. It has been said of gangster Legs Diamond that only his mother liked him, and she died when he was twelve. Certainly there were few criminals as cold-blooded as Diamond. Once, when police were after him and another gangster, Charles Entratta, for gunning down two hoodlums in the Hotsy Totsy Club in New York in 1929, Diamond and Entratta disappeared. Then Diamond launched a series of vicious murders to clear himself. First the bartender at the Hotsy Totsy, who had witnessed the murders, was shot to death, then, in quick succession, three customers who'd seen too much were also found murdered. The owner, a waiter, the cashier, and the hat check girl all disappeared, although it was hardly a mystery what had happened to them. The killing of two men had escalated to a total of ten murders. With everything now squared, Diamond and Entratta returned, saying they'd just heard they were wanted for something or other. They were tried for the original murders but because there were no eyewitnesses to testify against them, they were found not guilty. The Hotsy Totsy case, with the killing off of all witnesses, became a favorite plot of countless Hollywood movies.

2. Doing Penance. Queen Elizabeth I was perhaps the most lenient monarch in dealing with criminals if it meant an addition to the royal purse. When a wealthy landowner, John Copleston, murdered his godson in 1580, before the eyes of the entire congregation emerging from church, the only penalty the queen imposed was an order that Copleston plant an oak on the scene of the slaying. The Copleston Oak still stands in the churchyard of Tamerton Foliot, England. A less publicized aspect of the case was that Copleston also voluntarily handed over to the crown thirteen manorial estates.

3. The Defender. Ordered to have his arm chopped off for striking a foe at the court of Henry VIII, Sir Edmund Wyndham had only one request to make of his sovereign. He asked that his left arm be removed so he could continue to defend the king with his sword arm. Henry pardoned him.

4. The Shadow Knows. Some years ago, a Nebraska man was charged with dynamiting a house, and he beat the rap. Two astronomers, who did not meet each other, proved by independent calculations that he was innocent. Two girls had testified they had seen the defendant near the house not long before the explosion, which had taken place on a Sunday afternoon at exactly three o'clock. The girls had just left a church about a mile away at, they said, about two-thirty. They even produced a snapshot of themselves, taken as they left the church. Copies of the photograph were sent to the two astronomers, who were asked to determine the exact time it had been taken. They did this by measuring the shadow cast by one section of the church on another section. The two estimates were within fourteen seconds of each other, but both indicated the time was more than twenty-one minutes after the explosion had occurred. Their findings were confirmed by photos made on the same day the following year, and the man was freed.

5. Second Thought. In 1606, Prince Khusrau, the eldest son of Emperor Jehangir of India, was ordered to be blinded for having rebelled against his father. The prince was given the royal prerogative of inflicting the punishment on himself. He was supplied with a long steel needle and a torch, and received instructions on how to plunge the needle into his eyeballs. He was also given needle and thread with which to sew his eyelids shut after. The prince was locked in a chamber and kept there, screaming, until he had completed the gruesome task. When he pounded on the door, he was led, sightless, from the chamber. A year later, the emperor regretted the punishment he'd meted out to his son and called in the country's top physicians to restore his son's sight. When the threads on the prince's eyelids were removed, the doctors discovered his eyes were unharmed. After a few hours the prince could see normally. The prince had simply sewed his eyelids shut without thrusting the needle into his eyeballs, in the hope that someday his father would regret his orders.

Seven Incredible Escapes

1. Beg Pardon. The Most Polite Escaped Prisoner of the Decade award has to go to a Frenchman who broke out of a prison in Auxerre not too long ago. A few days after he went over the wall, the con, who had been doing a three-year term, sent the following postcard to the warden: "Everything is fine. Life is wonderful. Excuse the trouble I caused you." A later mail brought a tidy parcel containing his gray prison clothes—cleaned, pressed, and neatly folded.

2. The Rat. In 1907, Karl Schaarschmidt, a German with a record and a knack for breaking out of jail, was tucked into Gera Prison, from which officials knew he could never escape. His cell was specially constructed of thick masonry and huge oak beams. The cell door, three inches thick, had two locks on it that could not be reached from the inside through the aperture. The cell window had no bars that Schaarschmidt could file through but instead two heavy oak timbers; one was nine inches square, the other, seven. They were sunk deep in the masonry and formed a cross. The prisoner was given only a pewter spoon to eat with, and it was retrieved after each meal. Yet, five months later, Schaarschmidt shocked his jailers by breaking out through the cell window. How he'd done it wasn't explained until he was finally captured, two years later. The fugitive's front teeth were ground down to the gum line. Just as a trapped rat would do, Schaarschmidt had gnawed through the timbers to freedom.

3. Quiet, Please. The easiest escape of all time occurred in England during World War II when a twenty-three-year-old convict climbed over the wall of Pentonville Prison right before the eyes of the guards. The guards were powerless and neither rang the prison bell nor so much as blew their whistles. It was during the time when an invasion was feared and the ringing of bells and the blowing of whistles were to be the signal that the Germans had landed.

4. In Phones We Trust. Of all the ruses used to get out of jail, none ever matched the simplicity of the method employed by Léon Daudet to get out of Santé Prison in Paris. For years Daudet, a journalist, had characterized government officials as unthinking machines, and it no doubt gave them great satisfaction when they tucked him into Santé. Only five prisoners had ever escaped from Santé, built in 1867. Daudet simply had a friend call, pretend he was the minister of the interior, and say that Daudet had been pardoned. So unthinking was the warden that he immediately released his prisoner without checking the call.

5. Fooling the Doctors. By any standard, Charles W. Morse was a most successful swindler. Although he pulled hundreds of different swindles and took victims for millions, he was convicted only once, and even then he escaped punishment. Sentenced to fifteen years, Morse was given a full presidential pardon when doctors discovered he was terminally ill with Bright's disease. Morse lived happily ever after for another thirty years. Astonished doctors finally learned he had faked the disease by drinking a concoction composed mainly of soap.

6. Dirty Distractions. Sending prisoners saws to cut through their bars is an old ruse, but it was never executed with more resourcefulness than in the escape of Captain Charles Lux of French Intelligence from the German military fortress at Glatz. His brother sent him a faked passport concealed in a diary, as well as a dozen towels, which he could convert into a rope. The main problem was in the next shipment—a novel that concealed some saws and twenty-four gold coins. The book was so heavy it would have to provoke suspicion. Therefore the brother sent two other books. The warden promptly passed on the book with the contraband to Lux, but, predictably, he confiscated the other two books. They were filled with obscene drawings and pictures.

7. Reprieve. It took one of nature's most awesome disasters to free Henri Furcot, also known as Mal Henri. Mal Henri was arrested on a charge of murder early in May 1902 in St. Pierre, on the island of Martinique, in the West Indies. Furcot was imprisoned in the town's only jail, an old dungeon about three stories below the town hall, the only building in the city with subcellars. St. Pierre stood in the shadow of Mount Pelée, an active volcano. On May 6, 1902, Mount Pelée erupted, spewing forth hot lava, but since the eruption did not directly threaten the town, plans to evacuate St. Pierre were dropped. For two days the volcano continued to belch lava and ashes; then, suddenly, it erupted again, and a dense cloud of sulfurous gases settled heavily over all of St. Pierre and suffocated every living person and animal in the city, on the beach, and aboard every ship in the harbor. In all, 30,000 inhabitants and 10,000 holiday visitors died within three minutes. When rescuers arrived in St. Pierre, they found no survivors until they entered the old dungeon and found Mal Henri alive and breathing. The dungeon was so deep that the death-dealing gas had not reached him. Because of his incredible ordeal—and the fact that all records and witnesses in the case against him were gone—Mal Henri was released.

Five Strange Ways to Avoid Execution

Men facing imminent execution have often tried to save their lives in strange ways. Some succeed, others fail, and still others are saved only by incredible quirks of fate.

1. Glutton for Life. Most condemned men at Sing Sing welcomed the chance to get out in the exercise yard and slap a handball around, but not killer Donald Snyder. He never went near the yard. He devoted his exercise time, and virtually all his other time, to lying around in bed. And he ate every minute of the day. He transferred extra money he had to the death-house commissary to pay for extra food, and he never let the feed-up hack get away without overloading his tray. If gluttony were a capital offense, they would have had to execute Snyder twice. Snyder's strange behavior was finally explained when he told a guard, "I'm gonna get so fat, they won't be able to stuff me in the hot seat." Snyder weighed 150 pounds when he entered the death house, and by the date of his execution, July 16, 1953, he had ballooned to 300 pounds. When he was asked what he wanted for his last meal, he said, "Pork chops and eggs, and plenty of 'em." Naturally, this ingenious challenge to the electric chair was worthy of special newspaper coverage. As one New York newspaper summarized the execution, "The hot seat fitted him as though it had been made to order."

2. The Legal Way. The state reserves for itself the right to take a murderer's life and guards that right zealously. One may wonder why society doesn't allow a prisoner who is to be executed anyway to take his own life if he prefers to. But the state doesn't. Newspapers and magazines are collected each day to prevent a doomed man from rolling the papers into a crude club and hitting himself. Magazine staples are always removed because a desperate inmate might use one to puncture a vein or tear an artery. Toothbrushes are collected after each use because the handle might be sharpened into knifes. Yet, prisoners do try to find ways to beat the state at killing them. Johnny Reo is a Sing Sing death-row legend of sorts. While he was supposed to be sleeping he would snap off small pieces of bedspring and swallow them. For three weeks he continued to eat the metal, and only when the pain became unbearable did he stop. The pain made Reo scream in agony, but he refused to tell the prison doctor anything. X rays were taken and Reo was operated on. Besides six huge screws and two ounces of sand which Reo had scraped together in the exercise yard, twenty-five feet of bedspring were found inside him. Reo's life was saved but within a month he died in the chair. The same surgeon who had saved his life performed the autopsy after his death.

3. Card Trick of Death. When William Kogut entered San Quentin Penitentiary awaiting the death penalty, he openly boasted he would never be executed, that if he died, it would be by his own hand. As a result, guards kept an unusually close watch on him. Kogut's only diversion was playing solitaire with one of the two decks of cards he was allowed to keep in his cell. One Sunday morning, shortly before his slated execution, the prison was ripped by a terrific explosion.

Guards rushed to death row and found William Kogut lying in a pool of blood, his face a blob. Somehow Kogut had managed to kill himself. It took the coroner and a group of chemists days to figure out how he had done it. While ostensibly playing solitaire Kogut had shaved off all the red spots—the hearts and diamonds—with his thumbnail. He had then soaked them in water in his tin cup, producing a wet pulp. He wrenched a hollow knob from his cot and poured the pulp into the hollow knob and plugged the knob with a second knob so that it was airtight. Now Kogut had it—a potential deadly bomb. The bits of playing cards were made of cellulose and nitrate, which, when mixed with a solvent, formed pyroxylin, an explosive that is set off by heat. Kogut then built a tiny fire in his tin cup in some undetermined manner. He held his bomb over the flame until the pulp heated to the explosion point. Then he placed his face next to his bomb and just waited. Kogut's card trick can never be performed again. Condemned men are allowed playing cards in many prisons, but the decks are constantly collected and checked.

4. Jurisdictional Battle. On November 20, 1926, at the state penitentiary in Raiford, Florida, a convicted murderer, Jim Williams, was strapped in the electric chair. The electrodes were fitted and the black hood placed over his head. Williams tensed his body, but it was not racked by any lethal current. The warden and the sheriff got into an argument over whose duty it was to pull the switch. Warden Jackson had been known to feel that Williams had been convicted on the flimsiest of evidence and he'd often said he thought the man was innocent. The sheriff was equally adamant that he was not going to throw the switch. Indeed, he may have had doubts of his own about Williams' guilt. The argument raged for twenty minutes while the witnesses fidgeted. Finally, because no one would be the executioner, Williams was unstrapped and taken back to his cell. Reporters filed sympathetic stories, and for being subjected to twenty minutes of mental torture, Jim Williams had his sentence commuted to life imprisonment.

In time, Warden Jackson made Williams an honor prisoner, which gave him the chance to work outdoors on the state farm. One day in July 1934 Williams was working in the prison garden when he heard the guards shouting and cries of fear from an adjoining field. A woman and a teenage girl were being confronted by an enraged bull that was pawing the ground nervously, a sign that generally precedes an attack. Williams jumped over the fence and ran toward the women, ripping off his shirt. He waved it at the bull and the enraged beast charged at him instead of the terrified women. Williams almost made it to safety, but the bull gored him and flipped him into the air. Fortunately Williams landed on the other side of the fence. He had been gored in the thigh and both ankles were broken. For this act of heroism Williams won a full pardon and the gratitude of Warden Jackson, the man who had refused to execute him. The two women Williams had saved were the warden's wife and daughter.

5. Total Change. No man in history avoided execution and at the same time climbed to the heights that Michael II Psellus did. In the year A.D. 820, he was in a cell waiting for death when he heard the tramping of many feet. He expected the executioner but when a group of soldiers entered, they all kneeled before him. He was told that Emperor Leo V had been assassinated and that he had been chosen to succeed to the throne of the Eastern Roman Empire. Still wearing leg irons, Michael was carried to the coronation hall and crowned ruler of half the world.

Seven Tough-to-Kill Victims

1. The Iron Poet. Imprisoned in the Tower of London in 1613 at the instigation of Lady Frances Howard, the poet Sir Thomas Overbury was the object of a mighty murder campaign. Over a period of more than a hundred days he was fed a daily diet of arsenic, nitric acid, hemlock, ground diamonds, and mercury; he lived through it all, even though he should have died dozens of times over. Finally his guards were paid to kill Sir Thomas off with an injection of a powerful corrosive. The guards themselves were later executed.

2. Unkillable Sam. In post-Civil War New Orleans a black gravedigger named Samuel Dombey was hated by all the other black gravediggers because he worked for reduced rates. Finally the other gravediggers decided to eliminate the cut-rate competition. A delegation went to Dr. Beauregard, much feared for his potent black magic. Dr. Beauregard had what he called his "supreme curse," priced at fifty dollars, which would remove anybody. The delegation paid the money. Dr. Beauregard used an owl's head to curse the ground where Dombey was to dig a new grave the following day. The next morning, Dombey had barely started digging when there was a violent explosion in some nearby bushes. A man came staggering out, clutching his arm, and ran off. Dombey found an old shotgun, its breech shattered, in the bushes. Evidently someone had tried to shoot him. Fortunately for Dombey, the assassin had primed the old weapon with a very heavy charge of buckshot, and it had been too much for the old piece and the breech had blown up. A short time after that, Dr. Beauregard was walking with an arm in a sling and several patches on his face. He threatened to put a curse on anyone asking him why Sam Dombey was still digging graves.

The irate gravediggers next decided to handle the matter themselves. Dombey had a little toolhouse where he catnapped every afternoon. The men planted a keg of blasting powder under the cot, and after Dombey fell asleep someone slipped in and lit it. The blast completely destroyed the toolhouse, but Dombey who had been blown right out the door and landed some twenty feet away, amazingly was unhurt.

By this time the police at the station house had nicknamed him Indestructible Sam, and a short time later Dombey lived up to the name. Sam was taken prisoner by several masked men, put in a boat, and taken out on Lake Pontchartrain. Binding Sam hand and foot, they tossed him overboard in the inky darkness and headed for shore. In the part of the lake where they had dumped Sam, however, the water was only two feet deep. Sam waited till his would-be murderers were gone and then worked his hands and feet free and walked to shore. Next time, Sam's enemies set fire to his house; as he ran out he was shot full force in the chest with a buckshot charge. Firemen saved the house and got Sam to a hospital. This time it appeared Sam was destructible. But finally Sam pulled through. His body was pockmarked with scars from all the homicide attempts, but Sam kept on digging graves. Once a union was formed, gravedigging prices became uniform. But Sam won his personal battle. He lived into the twentieth century, dying at the age of ninety-eight. He had outlived all the old competitors who had tried to kill him.

3. Problems, Problems. Without a doubt, America's most frustrated murderer was Dr. Arthur Warren Waite, a New York dentist who had figured out a way to become a millionaire quickly. All he had to do was wipe out his wife's family. His wife was the only daughter of a wealthy drug manufacturer in Grand Rapids, Michigan. If Dr. Waite could hurry her parents' departure from this life, his wife would inherit a lot of money. Setting to work on his mother-in-law, Waite took her for a drive in a heavy rain with the windshield open. He put ground glass in her marmalade. He introduced into her food all sorts of bacteria and viruses—those that cause pneumonia, influenza, anthrax, and diphtheria. The lady did catch a cold, but that was all. In disgust, Waite shifted his attention to his father-in-law, trying the same disease producers—with absolutely no effect. He filled the old man's rubbers with water, dampened his sheets, opened a container of chlorine gas in his bedroom while he slept. Nothing. Then he tried giving the old man calomel, a purgative, to weaken him, and then a throat spray loaded with typhoid bacteria. People started commenting on how well the old man was looking. Waite got off the disease kick and switched to arsenic. Amazingly, the poison failed. Finally, Waite polished off the old man by smothering him with a pillow. By now, however, other relatives were suspicious, and an autopsy on the father-in-law's body was ordered. Heavy traces of arsenic were found; although this was not the cause of death, the arsenic was traced to Waite and he finally confessed to his crime.

4. Legs Diamond. There were many in the underworld who were convinced that Legs Diamond couldn't be killed. On at least four occasions he had been ventilated with bullets and survived. The first time was in October 1924, when a carload of men whom he was shaking down for some small change on petty rackets peppered his head with birdshot and put a bullet in his heel. Diamond drove to Mt. Sinai Hospital and was fixed up. Attack number two occurred on October 15, 1927, when rival gangsters knocked off Little Augie. They fired three shots into his aide, Diamond, for luck. Diamond was not expected to survive but he did. On October 13, 1930, gunmen invaded the cozy suite Legs was sharing with Kiki Roberts, a former show girl, and pumped four bullets into his body. Supposedly dying, he was taken to a hospital, where he proceeded to recover, to the absolute amazement of the surgeons and staff. Then, on April 26, 1931, he was cut down again as he was leaving a roadside inn. He took a bullet in the lung, another in the liver, another in the back, and a fourth in his arm. He was put down as a goner but survived again.

By this time Legs, too, was convinced he was immune to bullets. The popular saying was that he jingled as he walked. But on December 18 of that year two gunmen slipped into the room where he was sleeping and while one held him by the ears, the other shot him three times in the head. This time Legs was very dead.

5. The Suffering Husband. Albert Snyder, the victim in the the most famous murder case of the 1920s, was not killed on the first try. Twice his wife disconnected the gas while Snyder slept and then slipped from the room, shutting the door behind her. Both times the intended victim awoke and saved himself from asphyxiation. On another occasion, Ruth Snyder closed the garage doors on him with the motor of their automobile running. He almost succumbed to carbon-monoxide poisoning. Twice she tried doping his whiskey with bichloride of mercury but he poured it down the drain, commenting that it was rotten stuff and he would have to change bootleggers. Twice when Snyder was ill his wife substituted powerful narcotics for his medicine, but he survived.

After seven failures Mrs. Snyder turned to her lover, Judd Gray, for help. He agreed to aid her, and one evening, by appointment, he showed up at the Snyder home to commit murder. Albert Snyder worked late in his workshop in the basement and finally Gray left. A week later, Gray slipped into the house while the couple were out and saw a matchbox on the kitchen table. He was so drunk and tense at the time he couldn't remember if that was the signal that the murder was off or on. Finally he hid in the bedroom closet. When the Snyders came home, Gray waited until the husband was asleep and slipped out of the closet and hit the husband over the head with a sash weight. Snyder awoke and grabbed Gray by the necktie. Mrs. Snyder rushed to help Gray and, finally, blow after blow caused Snyder to sink into helplessness. Mrs.

Snyder then chloroformed her husband and drew some picture wire taut around his neck. The two lover-murderers couldn't keep to a straight story and were convicted of murder. Both died in the electric chair on January 12, 1928. Mrs. Snyder achieved an extra measure of fame when a reporter who had strapped a camera to his leg secretly snapped a picture of her as the current coursed through her body.

6. The Clay Pigeon of Chinatown.

Mock Duck was the greatest and most amazing character to emerge from Chinatown. Opium addict, gunman, killer, gambler, tong leader, and, eventually, elder statesman, Mock Duck for years dominated not only New York's Chinatown but also the ones in Boston and San Francisco. He led the Hip Sing Tong in its great wars with the On Leong Tong, the rich and powerful mob that had ruled New York's Chinatown until the appearance of Mock Duck. Nobody knows exactly how many times attacks were made on Mock Duck by his enemies or precisely how many men he killed, but he must have murdered at least a hundred people, and was himself attacked perhaps fifty times.

The first attack came a day after he told Tom Lee, the unofficial mayor of Chinatown and leader of the On Leongs, that he wanted half the revenues from all gambling and prostitution operations in Chinatown. Two prowling On Leongs caught up with him on a late-night stroll. They lunged at him with daggers and embedded them in Mock Duck's shoulders. He pulled loose, shot them, and ran back to the Hip Sing stronghold on Pell Street, the two knives still in his shoulders.

The next attack was another near miss. Mock Duck had sauntered out of his tong's headquarters right into the gun sights of a Chinese hatchet man. The first of the two shots grazed Mock Duck's coat. The second doubled him over and sent him reeling to the ground, clutching his stomach. Yet Mock Duck had escaped being hurt. The slug had struck his belt buckle, which was made out of a half-dollar.

This second attack convinced Mock Duck he needed protection. He consulted a Chinese ironmonger, who soon fashioned for him a bulletproof vest made of chain mail. Now Mock Duck searched for his enemies. Whenever he met four or five of them, he'd pull out two guns, squat, clamp his eyes shut, and start blazing away. Mock Duck was an awful shot. If he'd fired with his eyes open, his adversaries eventually would have discovered they could come at him, but when he shut his eyes and fired, their lives were in the hands of fate. Invariably they broke ranks and fled. On several occasions the chain-mail vest did protect Mock Duck from bullets and thrown hatchets.

The tong wars of Chinatown were noted for their intricate plots, but Mock Duck survived those against him. His foes did not fare so well. Ah Hoon, the celebrated Chinese comic of the day, was one of Mock Duck's most illustrious victims. A member of the On Leongs, he used his stage performances to poke fun at the Hip Sings and referred to Mock Duck as a "tub of lard." Angered, Mock Duck notified him that on December 30 he would die for his indiscretions. On the evening of his slated assassination, Ah Hoon appeared for his performance in the company of a police sergeant and two patrolmen, who sat onstage in full view of the audience. The theater was jammed, for all Chinatown wondered if Mock Duck would make good his threat. After the performance, still under police guard, the comic was hustled to the safety of his room in Chatham Square. On Leongs guarded his door—the room's only window faced a blank wall across a court—and then jubilantly spread the word that Mock Duck had failed to keep his pledge. The next morning, however, Ah Hoon was found shot to death. Mock Duck had lowered Sing Dock, another cunning Hip Sing killer, in a chair by a rope from the roof, and he had shot Ah Hoon through the open window with a gun that had a silencer.

Then there was the famous massacre at the Chinese Theater. It was packed to capacity on New Year's night, 1910, during a supposed truce between the tongs. But Mock Duck wasn't having any of that. The performance went along smoothly until someone in the audience suddenly hurled a bunch of lighted firecrackers into the air. This caused a brief commotion, then things settled down. When the audience filed out as the show ended, five men remained seated. They had bullets in their heads. Mixed in with the sounds of the firecrackers had been the revolver shots of five of Mock Duck's men. The police looked for Mock Duck immediately and found him at the local station house. At the moment of the killings Mock Duck had been complaining to the desk sergeant about a noisy neighbor.

In an effort to gain vengeance, the On Leongs were forever stalking Mock Duck, trying to catch him alone. Once, they caught Mock Duck without his guns. He had been drinking heavily and had lost them somewhere. On a Chinatown street a half-dozen On Leongs came at him, and Mock Duck sobered up fast. He rushed into a store, seized a ceremonial sword, and, yelling out to his men (who had apparently planned to meet there) to follow him, he charged out after the enemy, who broke and ran. Naturally, Mock Duck had no supporters in the store.

With every escape Mock Duck made, his stature grew in Chinatown. On many occasions the government of China, as well as the U.S. State Department, tried, without success, to stop the fighting in Chinatown. It was Mock Duck who stopped it in 1932 by announcing that he was going into retirement in a lavish home in remote Brooklyn. Peace at last reigned. Once a week until he died, in 1942, Mock Duck returned to Chinatown to visit his brother, who ran an importing firm on Pell Street. Mock Duck drove up in a limousine, which waited with motor running while he partook of a cup of tea and some dried octopus with his kin. About ten Hip Sing stalwarts stood guard around the building. There was no need for that. The On Leongs had no intention of attempting the impossible, trying to kill the legendary clay pigeon of Chinatown.

7. Iron Mike Malloy. Tony Marino's New York speakeasy at Third Avenue and 171st Street in the Prohibition days of 1932 was not exactly a gold mine. The liquor was lousy, the ambience only a little better, and, besides, people could get killed there. So Tony Marino developed a side business with his bartender, Joe Murphy, and two other friends, Dan Kreisberg and Frank Pasqua. It was the life-insurance business—not selling but collecting. Typical of how the gang operated was in the case of Betty Carlsen, a destitute ex-hairdresser who Marino learned had no money and no home. It was love at first sight. He gave her food and drink, and set her up in a furnished room around the corner. When Betty was in a deep stupor, Marino shoved paper and pen in her hand and told her to sign her name. He said it was a petition for some friend running for political office. Actually the paper was an insurance policy in which the soon-to-be-late Miss Carlsen was naming her new love as beneficiary. Then the gang drugged the girl, laid her out on the bed, poured ice water on her, and opened the windows to the mean March wind. Betty died of pneumonia and the boys collected.

They were looking for a fresh customer when Mike Malloy stumbled into Marino's place. Malloy was a bleary-eyed bum who seldom had the price of a drink but was always at the free food trays. Marino and Murphy were about to eject him when inspiration struck. Suddenly, Malloy was very welcome in the place. How about a free beer, Mike? How about another one? Pretty soon, the boys had a cot set up in the back room, where Malloy could sleep instead of in some drafty hallway. In time, Malloy signed a number of papers, including one that was an insurance policy, one that paid double in case of accidental death.

Then, one night, the boys got Malloy loaded to the gills and carried him out to the intersection of Baychester Avenue and Gun Hill Road in the Bronx. They carefully stretched him out and had a cabdriver, who was being paid $150 for his labors, run his taxi over him—not once but twice. The boys adjourned to Marino's to celebrate their coming good fortune. At eight-thirty the next morning, Fordham Hospital called to say that Mr. Malloy had been hit by a car and had asked that Mr. Marino be notified. He was in bad shape with a fractured collarbone, a slight concussion of the brain, and assorted bruises. He wouldn't be able to get back to Marino's for at least a week.

That fiasco made the boys decide to forget about the double-indemnity angle. It was important just to dispatch Mike Malloy as quickly as possible. He was drinking them out of house and home. So they decided to celebrate Malloy's return by serving him two dozen clams, soaked in wood alcohol. Malloy washed the clams down with a few mugs of beer and trotted off to his cot. The next day, Malloy was given more doctored clams. He loved them. Then Red Murphy came up with a concoction of six cans of antifreeze spiked with a small amount of gin. They offered it to Malloy as some new stuff that had just come in. Malloy loved it and told Marino that he would easily drive the other speaks in the area out of business by serving such wonderful booze. The next attack on Malloy was with a huge batch of poisoned sardines. Malloy downed four sandwiches at one sitting and asked for some of that "new booze" to go along with it. For three more days they fed him nothing but bad sardines, but Malloy not only didn't get ptomaine poisoning and die—he didn't even tire of them.

Were it not for the fact that the boys remembered the death of Betty Carlsen, they would have really been unhappy. So they got Malloy so drunk that he couldn't stand, took him to the far reaches of Crotona Park, and, stripping him of every stitch of clothing, dumped him unceremoniously into a snowbank and left him to freeze to death. Twenty-four hours later, Malloy was back, sporting a new suit. He explained that he must have tied one on and somehow had ended up clothesless in the park. When the police found him, they had to get the welfare people to outfit him before allowing him to return to society.

The saga of Mike Malloy ended, however, when the plotters finally decided on homicide, plain and simple, to do the deed. They rented a furnished room for him, ran a hose from a gas jet to his mouth, and on the night of February 22, 1933, Mike Malloy expired. But it was a messy kill. It meant bribing a doctor to sign a death certificate giving a different cause of death, and also there were too many loose tongues at work. The police started checking on an insurance-fraud ring at work in the Bronx and came up with the death of an Irishman named Malloy, who was buried within four hours after being certified dead. Atypically, there had been no wake. So Malloy's body was exhumed and the real cause of death determined. The doctor talked, the cabby talked, and the four plotters all died in the electric chair. One of the more humorously inclined New York papers could not resist speculating what would have happened if Mike Malloy had had to sit down in the chair; it was decided that he probably would have shorted the circuits at Sing Sing.

Six Bring-'Em-Back-Alive Cases

1. Front-Page Story. The best-known attempt in this country to bring an executed man back to life was a *Boston American* reporter's brainstorm. The reporter seeking to manufacture his own great scoop was Charles MacArthur, author of *The Front Page* and husband of Helen Hayes. MacArthur got the idea when he read a news story about a surgeon who had revived a baby who had been born dead. The operation consisted of opening the infant's chest, removing the heart, and massaging it gently until the baby resumed breathing. MacArthur consulted a surgeon friend and asked if the same could be done in the case of a man who had been hanged. The surgeon said yes, provided the man's neck was not broken and the body was brought to him within thirty minutes to an hour after the execution. MacArthur decided to try. He thought big—the financial rewards were limitless. There would be newspaper syndication of the story, a biography of the condemned man, movie rights, vaudeville and carnival rights, and book rights.

From among the four men then awaiting execution in Charleston, South Carolina, MacArthur picked out Paul Pappas, a thirty-year-old Greek fruit peddler who had been convicted of murder. He was thin, thus less likely to have his neck broken, and, best of all, spoke little English and couldn't spread the word about the plot. Pappas got his brother to sign over the legal ownership of the body to MacArthur. Next, MacArthur needed a way to get the assistant examiner to release the body quickly. He found the answer in a story that was making every paper from coast to coast. A young taxi driver had charged that a millionaire had forced him to have his procreative glands removed so that they could be transferred to the millionaire. MacArthur told the medic that Pappas was getting $5,000 to allow the same operation to be performed on himself for the benefit of a wealthy Bostonian. The money would go to Pappas' destitute family in Greece. The doctor agreed to pronounce the prisoner dead the minute he was cut down from the gallows. MacArthur's head was swimming with the expected success when, on the day of the execution, he began getting phone calls from many of Boston's leading doctors and surgeons, asking permission either to assist at or to observe the operation. MacArthur was frantic. He had told the surgeon not to breathe a word about the plot, but apparently the surgeon had told his colleagues. All MacArthur could do was pray that word didn't get back to prison officials.

MacArthur arranged for another reporter to cover the execution since he had to be outside to arrange for fast transportation of the body. Happily, he noted that the warden obviously knew nothing about the revival plot. Midnight, the time of the execution, came and passed. After ten minutes of nervous pacing MacArthur rushed into the courtyard just as reporters and witnesses were leaving. He demanded to know where the body was, and was told it had been taken to the infirmary. MacArthur raced there, and was greeted by the head medical examiner, wearing formal attire and with a broad smile on his face.

"No need to hurry, Charlie," the doctor said. "At a doctors' banquet tonight I heard two stories. One was that you intended to bring Pappas back to life. The other was that you only wanted his procreative glands. I decided the thing to do was to hurry over here. We're having Pappas autopsied right now. When it's over you can have the rest of him. The procreative glands will be usable, I believe."

Had MacArthur's secret been better kept, the reporter might have pulled off a unique coup in the annals of American journalism. Years later, MacArthur would write, "Whatever you do, never trust a woman or a doctor to keep a secret."

2. Legal Rub-out. Althought MacArthur's plot had failed, it triggered a series of similar attempts by condemned men. One such man was Salvatore Cardinella, or Il Diavolo, the leader of a ruthless gang in Chicago in the 1920s. Before his scheduled execution he went on a hunger strike and lost forty pounds. This loss of weight would, he hoped, enable his neck to survive the springing of the trap without being broken. Cardinella might have won his gamble with death had not authorities learned of the plot in advance. But a police lieutenant received a call from an informer belonging to a rival gang who had heard that Il Diavolo's relatives were going to revive him after the execution. The tip came only ten minutes before Cardinella was to die, and with three other officers the lieutenant hopped into a police car and sped to the prison just as a hearse pulled up. He opened the back door of the hearse and found a man and woman, dressed in white. What did a dead man need with a doctor and nurse? Inside the hearse was a rubber mattress filled with hot water, which was being heated by batteries. There were also an oxygen tent, stimulants, syringes, and twenty-four hot-water bottles. The lieutenant hurried into the prison and found Cardinella's body stretched out on a slab. His relatives had signed the papers that gave them possession of the body, but the officer announced that the corpse could not be moved until morning. The dead man's relatives cursed and threatened him, but the body stayed put. Later investigation showed that Cardinella might have been revived if heat had been applied to the body soon enough.

3. The Sure Thing. In eighteenth-century Ireland some English hangmen developed a most profitable sideline by doing a bad job of carrying out an execution. The hangman was required to stand beneath the gallows and, as the condemned man swung from the noose, pull down on the victim's legs to make sure of death. Often the condemned man's relatives or friends asked permission to do that grim chore themselves so as to assure the hanged man's suffering ended as quickly as possible. If, however, the hangman was paid enough, he might look away while this was supposedly being done; instead the prisoner's friends would hoist the body up to relieve the pressure on the neck. Then the man would be cut down, placed in a coffin, and carted away. One man who so survived, a Mr. O'Brien, later was caught again and executed for a new offense. This time there was to be no revival. As O'Brien was about to be cut down an officer stepped forward and applied the coup de grâce with a bullet in the brain.

4. No Help. There are cases on record of condemned men surviving hangings with no outside assistance. William Duell, a seventeen-year-old robber, was hanged at Tyburn Prison, London, on November 29, 1740. Duell was one of five prisoners hanged on the same day. After he had dangled for twenty-two minutes, he was ordered cut down by Sheriff John Hoare. Carted off to Surgeons' Hall to be dissected, Duell came back to life when a servant began washing the body. The servant noticed labored breathing and called the doctors. They bled Duell, since bleeding was then one of the most popular forms of medical treatment for practically any ailment. Through, or perhaps in spite of, the treatment, Duell was able to sit up within two hours, although he was still unable to speak. Doctors notified Sheriff Hoare, but by that time it was several hours after the execution. The sheriff decided to string Duell up again. But word of what had happened had spread and a huge crowd had gathered. They threatened to hang the sheriff if he attempted to rehang Duell. Sheriff Hoare was kept trapped in the hall until after midnight. He finally returned Duell to his cell and waited for his superiors to decide what to do.

The duke of Newcastle, the secretary of state, did not know how to handle the matter and ordered that nothing be done until he could study a full written report. Meanwhile, the sensational London press had a field day. Bogus interviews with Duell were published in which he told of all the ghosts he'd seen while dangling from the gallows.

Meanwhile, the experts couldn't agree what had gone wrong. Some doctors said Duell, at 125 pounds, simply had not been heavy enough. They recommended that a fifty-pound weight be tied to his feet. Other doctors said Duell should have been left hanging longer. One noted that Duell had been suffering from a high fever since his conviction and that this fever had sped up the circulation of the blood so much that the noose had not been able to halt it. The king himself became so intrigued with the botched hanging that he had the royal physicians investigate. Their opinion was that the hangman had been careless in adjusting the noose.

Whatever the reason, the king ruled that Duell was not to be hanged again. He ordered that Duell be transported instead, and the man who beat the noose was sent to the New England colonies in America.

5. Slow Burn. It is a scientifically accepted fact that a man executed in the electric chair can sometimes be brought back to life. As long as doctors can revive men electrocuted by live wires, it is also often possible to save a man who has had a lethal jolt in the chair. Because of this possibility, most states with the electric-chair death penalty have passed laws that require all electrocuted persons to be subject to an immediate autopsy. One thing is certain: These men stay dead. One man who lived for a while after being subjected to the chair is Fred Van Wormer, who was executed at New York's Dannemora Prison. After the executioner had reached home, he received a call to return immediately. It turned out that as Van Wormer's body lay in the autopsy room, guards saw it suddenly start to move. Van Wormer was not dead, although he had been so declared. It didn't seem right to perform an autopsy on someone still alive. By the time the executioner returned to the scene, however, Van Wormer had, for certain, expired. Nonetheless, his lifeless body was lugged back to the chair and charged with another jolt of 1,700 volts.

6. The Half-Hanged Man. The man who became known as Half-Hanged Smith is John Smith, an eighteenth-century English sailor and soldier who took up burglary on his return to civilian life. He was caught and sentenced to death. From the beginning, Smith predicted he would never hang, since men with long military-service records were at times rewarded with the king's pardon. By the time he was taken to Tyburn, however, Smith began to have his doubts. As the noose was being placed around his neck Smith cried, "His majesty had better hurry up or he'll lose one of the best defenders the crown ever had."

The hangman hoisted him high. Smith had been dangling for fifteen minutes when the king's horseman came riding up. He had a reprieve for Smith. The executioner hurriedly cut Smith down; he was taken to a nearby house, where doctors labored over him and finally brought him to consciousness. Smith was returned to a prison cell, and two months later, because of his ordeal on the gallows, was given a full pardon.

Smith was not one to take advantage of his good fortune. Within a few months he was arrested again, but since the case against him was weak, he was acquitted. Within a short time he was arrested for a third offense. This time the prosecutor died before the case came to court, and eventually the case was dropped. In an age of superstition, many people believed Smith when he said he could not be hanged. The London underworld considered him immortal—until he was honored at a party after his latest release. In a bitter twist no writer of fiction would dare employ, Half-Hanged Smith choked to death on a fishbone.

XII.
CRIMES AND PEOPLE: THEY WORK IN MYSTERIOUS WAYS

Eight Crimes That Never Were

1. The Empty Graves. A bizarre "murder plot" came to light back in the early 1920s in Hammond, Indiana. A sixty-nine-year-old man was informed by his twenty-three-year-old bride that she was pregnant. The man was wildly happy because he had desperately wanted his wife to give him a child. Some months later, the wife was assisted at home by a woman friend in giving birth not to one baby but to two. The babies, however, named Loren and Lorene, were so weak and susceptible to germs that the father was never permitted to see them. He had to be content to stand outside the bedroom door and listen to them cry. This strange arrangement went on for about a year, when the wife told her husband the babies were very ill. She rushed off with them to Chicago so they could receive special medical treatment. Returning a week later, she informed her husband that the children had died and been buried in Chicago. Suspicious that the wife had murdered the children, the husband went to the police. The wife was arrested on a murder charge when she was unable to say where the children were buried. She was freed at her trial, however, for her lawyer proved she had concocted the whole story. She had never even been pregnant but had made up the entire story to stop her husband's nagging for children. She had gone to Chicago so that she could conclude the deception. As final proof, the lawyer presented Loren and Lorene—two crying dolls.

2. Surrounded by Death. Some years ago, in a small English rural community, there was a series of strange deaths. Whole families were wiped out by a mysterious ailment doctors could not identify. The local police finally called in Scotland Yard for assistance, for they reluctantly had concluded that the unexplained mass deaths could be the work of a master criminal. But the intervention of Scotland Yard did not frighten off the unknown killer. The death toll continued to mount, and all leads proved fruitless. Autopsies revealed nothing. Violent cramps and nausea hit persons who had never been sick a day in their lives. Yet there were some houses in which there were no illnesses or deaths. That fact eventually produced the solution. Most of the "healthy" houses had painted interiors rather than wallpaper. The wallpaper proved to be the culprit.

It was learned that a certain wallpaper manufacturer had sold a considerable amount of his product in the area, and many houses contained it. The wallpaper had arsenical dyes in it. No ill effects from it developed immediately, but, years later, when people repapered their homes, the paste under the new paper underwent a process of fermentation, which liberated small amounts of hydrogen gas, harmless in itself. In time, the hydrogen gas set up a chemical reaction with the arsenical dyes of the old paper and formed arsine, which is a lethal gas. With this discovery, the strange rash of deaths ended. Today, most countries, including the United States, prohibit the use of arsenical dyes in wallpaper.

3. The Impossible Suicide. One evening, neighbors of a young Cleveland couple heard an hour-long argument that was finally punctuated with a gunshot and called the police. They arrived on the scene within a few minutes and found the young wife lying across her bed, fully clothed, with a wound above her heart and her right arm flung backward. A gun was found behind a trunk that stood against a wall a good ten feet away. The husband swore that his wife had committed suicide, but after the medical examiner arrived and removed not one but two bullets from the woman's heart, the husband was placed under arrest. The police reasoned that one couldn't shoot oneself twice in the heart and then hide the gun ten feet away before falling down to die. After a more thorough study, however, including a detailed inspection of the peculiar shapes of the bullets and the fact that there was only one bullet hole, scientists realized that the husband had been telling the truth after all. The first bullet had been fired from the gun sometime before but had stuck in the barrel. It was knocked out when the second bullet was fired and they traveled as one into the woman's heart. Because the barrel had been stopped up, obstructed gas had caused a terrific recoil, which had wrenched the gun from the woman's hand and lodged it in its seeming hiding place behind the trunk.

4. The Impossible Murder. An elderly businessman wanted his young wife and small children to benefit from his large life-insurance policy, which did not pay in the event of suicide, and so he planned his own "murder." He turned his Cleveland business office into a shambles, pulling out drawers, scattering papers. He smashed his wristwatch, tore an expensive ring off his finger, emptied the money out of his wallet, and tossed the leather case into a corner. He punched the wall hard so that he bruised his hand as though he had struck his assailant in the skull. Then he fired two shots into a wall. The third bullet he put in his brain. His idea was to make the police conclude that a thief had killed him and had tried to make it look like suicide until he had been frightened off. The medical examiner was fooled for all of five seconds before he told the officers that he suspected suicide. The officers were not convinced. Wasn't it possible that a murderer had held a gun against his head and shot him?

"Try taking the gun out of his hand," the doctor said.

The man's fingers were wrapped tightly around the butt. This phenomenon is known as cadaver spasm, and it can occur only at the moment of death. It is a sure sign of suicide or accident, although its absence does not necessarily mean murder. There is no way to fake such a spasm, since the fingers of a dead person cannot be forced to tighten. The police soon found the financial motive for the suicide, and in the drain in the men's room they found three torn-up ten-dollar bills and the man's ring.

5. Suicide on the Rebound. Another man who wished to commit suicide and make it look like murder turned his pockets inside out and then shot himself in his private garage. He was found sprawled there, an obvious murder victim, since there was no gun. One sharp-eyed detective was not convinced, however. He noticed a deep, fresh gouge near the top of a wall, one that did not quite reach the ceiling. The wall concealed some open piping. But when the officer looked behind the wall, he found more than pipes. He also discovered the gun. It was hanging from a rubber strap that was tied around a pipe. The man had obviously pulled the gun into the garage area and shot himself in the brain. When the gun dropped from his hand, the band had snapped it over the wall and out of sight.

6. The World's Most Dangerous Voice. Probably the strangest crime ever charged to any person was the one leveled against Elizabeth Billington, who has been described as the greatest singer England ever produced. On May 30, 1794, in Naples, Italy, she sang in *Inez di Castro,* an opera written especially for her powerful voice. Two weeks later, Mount Vesuvius erupted, and Neapolitans were sure that her singing had caused it. The populace became so enraged that the singer had to flee the city to avoid being lynched.

7. The Street-Corner Slaying. One of the most ironic miscarriages of justice occurred in Philadelphia. A young man who had met his girlfriend one evening on a street corner was alleged to have argued with her and hit her across the back of the neck with a beer bottle. The prosecution produced three witnesses who said they had observed the assault. The jury ignored the man's story that he had merely embraced the girl and was stroking the back of her neck when suddenly she lurched against him and collapsed on the sidewalk, blood spurting from her mouth. The "killer" had served three years of a life sentence before it was proved that the girl had really died because of an aneurysm in the aorta; in this heart condition the blood vessel can burst, fatally, at any moment. Shock or excitement can cause the rupture. Only after this medical fact was uncovered did the three supposed eyewitnesses admit that they really hadn't seen a beer bottle in the man's hand. They "had thought that he had something in his hand" and assumed that he and the girl had argued, although they hadn't heard the conversation.

8. The Lady Killer. One misty night in 1921, two police officers spotted a man with two large burlap-wrapped packages near Brooklyn's India Wharf. Before they could stop him, he heaved one into the water. Then they seized him before he could jettison the other. They opened the package and found a pair of woman's arms. The man, Travia, told of having picked up a woman in a bar and taking her to his rooms. They had both been drinking heavily. When she demanded more to drink, as well as money, he had slapped her around and knocked her to the floor. Then he'd stretched out on the bed and gone to sleep. He awoke some hours later. The lights were blazing and he had a terrific headache. When he got out of bed he tripped over the woman's body. She was dead. He realized he had killed her. Thinking fast, he got a knife, a chisel, and a small cleaver and started chopping up her body. He had been caught dumping the first parts, the limbs.

Travia led the police to his place, where he showed them a headless torso. The head lay several feet away, near a coal-burning iron stove. The face was an eerie, cherry-red color. The police had the case wrapped up neatly—the body, the killer, the confession—by the time the chief medical examiner, Charles Norris, arrived. He took one look at the scene and said, "You've got an innocent man, boys." The cherry-red color of the face suggested carbon-monoxide poisoning. An autopsy confirmed it. The woman's brain was loaded with alcohol and she had been in a stupor. Travia had closed the window and lit the coal stove when they came in. Carbon monoxide from the stove accumulated in the unventilated room and was enough to kill the woman. Travia, who had not downed as much liquor as his lady friend, woke up before the gas could have the same deadly effect on him. When he awoke, he remembered having argued with her and assumed he had killed her. Travia walked out of a court hearing a free man but had further trouble with the law. He was issued a summons for transporting a body through the streets without a permit.

Comments by Eight Witnesses Who Didn't Help Kitty Genovese

Early in the morning of March 13, 1964, thirty-seven respectable, law-abiding citizens in Queens, New York City, watched a killer stalk and then stab a young woman in three separate attacks over a period of thirty-five minutes—and not one even called the police. The victim was twenty-eight-year-old Kitty Genovese. Stabbed at three-twenty A.M. by twenty nine-year-old Winston Moseley, she screamed out, "Oh, my God, he stabbed me! Please help me! Please help me!" Several lights went on in a ten-story apartment house across the street. From one of the upper windows a man yelled, "Let that girl alone!" Moseley looked up at the man, shrugged, and walked down Austin Street where his car was parked. Lights went out.

The killer then returned to the girl, who was now trying to crawl to the building in which she lived. He stabbed her again. "I'm dying!" she screamed. "I'm dying!" The lights went on again and windows were opened. The assailant climbed into his car and drove off. Kitty Genovese staggered to her feet and tried to make it to a nearby hallway. It was now three-thirty-five A.M. Again the assailant returned, got out of his car, and started searching doorways for his victim. He found her in a hallway at the foot of a staircase. He stabbed her for a third time—fatally. It was three-fifty before the police got their first call. They were there in two minutes but were too late.

Eventually, murderer Moseley was caught. But police, reporters, and psychologists were interested in why nobody had called the police earlier, when Kitty Genovese could have been saved. Here are some comments from some of the witnesses who would talk.

1. "I didn't want to get involved."

2. "We thought it was a lovers' quarrel."

3. "Frankly, we were afraid."

4. "I didn't want my husband to get involved."

5. "I don't know."

6. "I was tired. I went back to bed."

7. "The last time I complained to police, I was sent to a concentration camp."

8. "Get away or I'll throw you down the steps."

And what of the man who finally did call the police? Before he did so, he telephoned a friend in Nassau County to ask his advice on what he should do.

Four "Postmortems"

1. Murder Ghouls. The most gruesome aspect of many murders is not the crime itself but the sickening fact that many persons want to collect souvenirs. One of the most shocking cases was that of the 1827 murder of a young girl, Maria Marten. A maniac had killed her in a barn on a farm in Suffolk, England. Thousands of collectors came from all over the United Kingdom. They descended on the farm and completely demolished the barn. The hundreds who arrived too late to grab a piece of the barn made off with anything they could find nearby, including sticks and stones.

2. The Remains of Bonnie and Clyde. After Bonnie Parker and Clyde Barrow were ambushed by the law and killed, hundreds of people gathered at the scene of the car they'd died in. Bonnie's dress was almost cut from her back by souvenir hunters. The same happened to Clyde's bloodied shirt and undershirt. People clipped away at Bonnie's hair, and one person was trying to remove the diamond rings from her fingers when the coroner and undertaker arrived and stopped him. Every piece of glass was picked up from the road; others wanted a hubcap. Trees were cut down so that bullets could be dug out of them. One man tried to cut off Clyde's ear. He said he wanted to preserve it in alcohol. When the bodies were brought to Dallas, 20,000 people jammed the street in front of the funeral home in which Bonnie's body lay, and as many came to view Clyde. Hot-dog and soda-pop vendors had a field day. The funerals, a few days later, were nightmares as the crowds took over. Airplanes swooped low and dropped flowers on the biers. Barrow's sister couldn't get through the crowds and never got to within forty feet of the grave.

3. The Costello Legacy. When syndicate boss Frank Costello died, his widow was determined that nothing would mar the dignity of his funeral. Almost no one was there whom the police might have an interest in. The funeral and burial were the epitome of dignity. Then, as the widow turned to leave the burial site, a cousin whom she apparently didn't know or didn't recognize approached, hat in hand. Mrs. Costello leaned forward to hear the expected condolences. "What are you going to do with Frank's clothes?" he whispered. Mrs. Costello walked on without answering.

4. A Visit to Son of Sam. After the capture of New York's Son of Sam, the killer's Yonkers apartment became a landmark—a madness museum for curiosity hunters who came to gawk, tear out shreds of the carpeting he'd walked on, and scream his name. In the middle of the night, people came by and shouted, "David, come out." Souvenir hunters traipsed through the apartment house, stealing doorknobs as mementos and chipping pieces of paint from the door of the alleged .44-caliber killer. David Berkowitz's old apartment remained vacant. The desperate landlord changed the address of the house from 25 to 42 Pine Street to protect the tenants. By the beginning of 1978, however, over 25 percent of the building's tenants had moved out.

Seven Strange Tales of Animals in the World of Crime

1. The Avenging of Nails Morton. The "rubbing out" of a horse by the underworld was made famous in Mario Puzo's *The Godfather*. But its real-life counterpart was perhaps equally gruesome.

Samuel J. "Nails" Morton was one of the top guns of Dion O'Banion's North Side Chicago mob. Morton was looked upon with awe by other gangsters because he had won the *Croix de Guerre* in France and had come back after World War I as a first lieutenant. The mob was convinced that Nails could never be gunned down by rival gangsters, and they were right. He was thrown by a horse and kicked to death in Lincoln Park.

The O'Banion gang, determined on vengeance, in true mob style kidnapped the horse at gunpoint from the riding stable and took the animal to the spot where Nails had been killed. The horse was bumped off when each gangster solemnly shot the poor beast in the head.

2. Jailbait. Perhaps the most unusual witness in a criminal case was a shark that was harpooned near the coast of Jamaica in 1799.

An American vessel, the *Nancy*, was seized by a British naval vessel on suspicion of carrying contraband. Before British sailors could board the *Nancy*, however, its crew managed to jettison the smuggled goods and the captain heaved the ship's papers over the side in a weighted pouch. The captain had a fake set of papers on hand that indicated the ship was on an innocent mission. The captain and crew were brought to trial at Port Royal, but it was soon apparent they were going to be acquitted because of the lack of incriminating evidence. But just as the prosecution was about to sum up its case, the captain of another ship entered the court with the *Nancy*'s original papers. His men had harpooned a shark that morning and, upon cutting open its belly, had found the pouch and the incriminating documents from the *Nancy*. The smugglers were convicted and the evidence was exhibited thereafter at the Institute of Jamaica, in Kingston.

3. Murder Steer. In Brewster County, Texas, back when they settled arguments about cattle ownership with lead, a group of men got into a hassle about a single steer. When the smoke had cleared, six men were dead. The deaths, at least, had a sobering effect. The steer was branded, in capital letters, with the word "murder," and lived out its days as a grim reminder of the tragedy.

4. The Hairy Man. During a storm in the North Sea in 1705 a small ship sank off the English coast, near the village of West Hartlepool. The only survivor was a pet ape that had belonged to a member of the crew. The animal, washed ashore on a beam, had been found by fishermen. The villagers had never seen an ape and, since they were at war with the French, quickly decided the strange man was a French spy. Obviously, his hairy disguise and weird chattering were intended to fool them. The animal was brought to trial and sentenced to hang. A number of people were hoping the condemned man would make a confession on the gallows, but his last words were only more animallike chattering.

5. The Deadly Camel. In the mid-eighteenth century the sultan of Morocco trained a royal camel to be the executioner. When a man was condemned to death, he was thrown into a courtyard. The trained camel quickly would seize him with its powerful teeth, raise him high in the air, slam him to the ground, and then kneel on him until the life was crushed out of him.

6. Suing Insects. For the five hundred years preceding the eighteenth century, a large number of lawyers made a handsome living by persuading ignorant peasants to bring troublesome insects to trial so that depredations against crops would stop. The trials were long-drawn-out affairs, and the delays increased court costs and, of course, the lawyers' fees. In 1445 the inhabitants of St. Julian, France, started action against a swarm of insects. The case dragged on, bleeding the peasants, then their children, then their grandchildren, until, after fifty years, the case was finally dropped. It was by then apparent that if the insects had been ignoring official subpoenas for five decades, they were never going to appear in court to face the charges against them.

7. The Parrot Stoolie. The Green Parrot Bar and Restaurant, on New York's Upper East Side, had an extra-added attraction besides generous portions of liquor. There was also proprietor Max Geller's pet parrot, which was a very talented bird. It would greet a number of patrons by name, but, more importantly, it had a varied, if salty, vocabulary and could regale them with entertaining insults. It could also yell out; "It's murder."

On the night of July 12, 1942, that was the phrase the bird should have been using when police were summoned. Geller lay behind the bar, mortally wounded, and the hysterical parrot kept screaming, "Robber, robber." Patrons at the bar said they had not noticed who had last entered and was talking to

Geller. Hearing shots, they looked up and saw a figure fleeing. The police were faced with a number of witnesses who couldn't or wouldn't talk and a parrot who wouldn't shut up. The bird kept on yelling, "Robber, robber."

The Geller case stayed unsolved for two years, when a detective still assigned to the case had a brainstorm. The bird had been trained to call patrons by name. What if the parrot had not been saying the word "robber" after all? It had been hysterical and could have been mangling the word. What if the bird had really been saying, "Robert, Robert"?

The police backtracked and discovered there had been a regular patron whose name was Robert. He had disappeared about the time of the Geller killing. Eventually the man was arrested in Baltimore, and confessed to the murder—which remains the only one on record that has been solved by a parrot.

Ten Legal Rulings

1. It's ruled a murder if you keep a foot locker in the basement, warn your wife never to look in it, and then set up a booby trap with dynamite that kills her when she disobeys you. That's a cunning way to murder the wife because it put her under a psychological strain she couldn't possibly deal with.—*Oregon court*

2. If you threaten your wife that you will beat her up and she jumps in the river to avoid your attack and then drowns, that's judged murder—"a deliberate and diabolical intention to force his wife to her death."—*Supreme Court of New Jersey*

3. If you shoot a man in a way that will be fatal but he then kills himself before your bullets can kill him, you're still guilty of murder. The suicide did not really stop the bullets from killing the man but, rather, hurried their work. —*Supreme Court of California*

4. It's homicide if you hold up a gas station and the attendant takes a shot at you and kills a bystander by accident. "When a felon sets in motion a chain of events he should be held responsible for any death which results from his criminal act."—*Supreme Court of Pennsylvania*

5. If your wife catches you putting arsenic in her food, you cannot stop her from testifying against you just because she is your wife. A wife is barred from revealing only those confidences her husband shares with her.—*Kentucky Court of Appeals*

6. If you know that sleep is necessary to save your uncle's life and you keep telephoning him all night until he dies, it's ruled a murder. Nervous irritation can have the same deadly effect as a gun or knife.—*Supreme Court of Idaho*

7. If you bang your wife around and she calls a doctor and he tells her to take a drink of brandy and it accidentally goes down her windpipe and kills her, you are guilty of homicide. "The blow rendered the application of the brandy necessary and the defective swallowing was the consequence of the blow."—*Supreme Court of Pennsylvania*

8. If your wife decides to run off with another man and robs you at gunpoint so that they will have enough money, she is guilty of armed robbery. A husband and wife generally are no longer considered a single entity in the eyes of the law, and each can be guilty of robbing the other.—*Ohio court*

9. If your girlfriend stabs you and you would have survived except for the fact that you overate during your recovery, she is still guilty of murder. A stabbed man is not bound to eat wisely just so his assailant can be free of a murder charge.—*Alabama Court of Appeals*

10. If you smack a man over the head with a bottle at a party and he is hospitalized and dies when he catches scarlet fever from a nurse he tries to kiss, you are not guilty of manslaughter. "The scarlet fever came by a visitation of Providence and not from the act of the party inflicting the blow."—*Supreme Court of Kentucky*

Big Bestsellers from SIGNET

- ☐ **LILY CIGAR** by Tom Murphy. (#E8810—$2.75)*
- ☐ **BALLET!** by Tom Murphy. (#E8112—$2.25)*
- ☐ **TWO NYMPHS NAMED MELISSA** by John Colleton. (#E8848—$2.25)*
- ☐ **SWEETWATER SAGA** by Roxanne Dent. (#E8850—$2.25)*
- ☐ **JUST LIKE HUMPHREY BOGART** by Adam Kennedy. (#J8820—$1.95)*
- ☐ **THE DOMINO PRINCIPLE** by Adam Kennedy. (#J7389—$1.95)
- ☐ **LOVE SONG** by Adam Kennedy. (#E7535—$1.75)
- ☐ **CITY OF WHISPERING STONE** by George Chesbro. #J8812—$1.95)*
- ☐ **SHADOW OF A BROKEN MAN** by George Chesbro. (#J8114—$1.95)*
- ☐ **WINGS** by Robert J. Serling. (#E8811—$2.75)*
- ☐ **PHOENIX** by Amos Aricha and Eli Landau. (#E8692—$2.50)*
- ☐ **THE GODFATHER** by Mario Puzo. (#E8970—$2.75)
- ☐ **EYE OF THE NEEDLE** by Ken Follett. (#E8746—$2.95)*
- ☐ **DEATH TOUR** by David J. Michael. (#E8842—$2.25)*
- ☐ **JO STERN** by David Slavitt. (#J8753—$1.95)*

*Price slightly higher in Canada

Buy them at your local bookstore
or use this convenient coupon for ordering.

THE NEW AMERICAN LIBRARY, INC.,
P.O. Box 999, Bergenfield, New Jersey 07621

Please send me the SIGNET and MENTOR BOOKS I have checked above. I am enclosing $_____ (please add 50¢ to this order to cover postage and handling). Send check or money order—no cash or C.O.D.'s. Prices and numbers are subject to change without notice.

Name _____

Address _____

City _____ State _____ Zip Code _____

Allow at least 4 weeks for delivery
This offer is subject to withdrawal without notice.